Old-Time Brand-Name Desserts

Old-Time Brand-Name Desserts

Recipes, Illustrations, and Advice
from the Recipe Pamphlets of America's
Most Trusted Food Makers

BUNNY CRUMPACKER

SMITHMARK

Acknowledgments

For enthusiastic recipe testing, great thanks to Jody Richards, who swims in the Hudson River, and to Lynda Johnson, on an island in Puget Sound. My thanks too to testers Cassidy Cokeley and Louise Rogers. I'm very grateful to two Joannes, both of whom lent me books: JoAnn Shaheen, for her grandmother's copy of "The Monarch Iron Range Book," and Joanne Rubin, who sent "More Work for Mother." Love and thanks to Chick and Casey Crumpacker, who tasted *everything*.

This edition published in 1999 by SMITHMARK Publishers, a division of U.S. Media Holdings, Inc., 115 West 18th Street, New York, NY 10011.

SMITHMARK books are available for bulk purchase for sales promotion and premium use. For details write or call the manager of sales, SMITHMARK Publishers, 115 West 18th Street, New York, NY 10011; 212-519-1300.

ISBN 0-7651-1653-7

10987654321

Library of Congress Catalog Card Number: 99-75818

Designer: Kay Schuckhart/Blond on Pond
Photography: Peter Carr

Printed in Singapore

BLUE LABEL MENUS

Contents

*M*ost of us look forward to dessert. It's taken into consideration well before it occurs. After all, dessert is not casual. It doesn't just happen. The right dessert involves choice and planning and imagination and hope. If a good meal were a story, dessert would be the last word, the "amen." Dessert concludes, it punctuates, it's the exclamation point,

Eat Dessert First

the period. Dessert is a coda, a full stop, a happy ending. Dessert is the taste you're left with, and it's the first memory of a meal you've already eaten.

There are people who eat dessert for the same reason other people climb a mountain: because it's there. There are others, sweet souls, who see beyond the obvious. They

recognize dessert for what it is — a dream, a delight, a virtue, a reward. I ate my vegetables; now, I want my dessert. *Give me my dessert!*

Into which category do I fall? For a long time, in restaurants, given a menu, I'd choose dessert first. Then I'd plan the rest of the meal. Now, I'm more moderate. I choose the appetizer first; *then* I decide on dessert. The middle either falls into place or it can be dispensed with altogether. This is a menu philosophy that goes with the T-shirt advice, "Life is short. Eat dessert first."

Desserts are made with just a few basic ingredients: sugar (the *sine qua non*), butter, flour, milk, flavoring, and perhaps some fruit. If it seems strange that these precious few ingredients can be combined and recombined to create so many wonderful and different desserts, consider that just the twenty-six letters of the alphabet are enough for both Shakespeare *and* the Marx Brothers, and only ten digits are enough to count everything in the universe.

Aside from cholesterol and the sugar blues (a small worry if one can manage to eat in moderation), desserts can be close to perfect. But even so, cooking is not about perfection. Cooking is about imagination, taste, history, tradition, spirit, and, when you're lucky, love. It surely would be a sadder world without the sweetness of dessert.

From Yesterday's Kitchens

All the recipes in this book, like those in my first book, *The Old-Time Brand-Name Cookbook,* are based on cooking pamphlets issued by food manufacturers in the years from 1875 to 1950. The time span encompassed by these recipe pamphlets begins with the late Industrial Revolution, and reaches to the beginnings of the truly modern kitchen, just after World War II. At the beginning of that three-generation span, the first processed foods were introduced. Such products of the Industrial Revolution as packaged yeast, powdered gelatin, and baking powder are foods we take for granted today. We don't even think of them as processed, though they are.

For cooks in the last quarter of the nineteenth century, those first processed foods were miracles of convenience and speed. Before then, cooking was incredibly tedious and time-consuming. In order to make something as simple as a gelatin dessert, for instance, long hours had to be spent boiling beef and veal bones for a stock sufficiently strong and reduced to gel. There were no refrigerators, no gas or electric stoves, no canned or frozen foods. The beef bones for gelatin were cooked over an iron range that burned wood or coal — and that in itself was an advance from cooking over an open hearth.

In order to heat the iron stove, the cook had to shovel out the cold ashes, build a new fire, replenish it, and guess at the temperature (by holding her hand in the oven, or, as one household hint of the day had it, by putting a piece of paper in the oven and noting how quickly it turned brown and began to burn). Once the right temperature (or thereabouts) was reached, it had to be maintained, and when all the cooking was done and the stove was cold, the cook had to polish it with blacking to make it clean again. And before she cooked another meal, she had to go out and chop the wood — or shovel the coal — for the next fire. It is with good reason that Charles Dickens called the first cast-iron stoves red-hot monsters.

Similarly, the ice box was an advance over the cold cellar: It was a convenience but it still meant enormous amounts of work. Ice had to be delivered with some frequency, and when it melted, the drip-pan had to be emptied promptly. The inside of the ice box wasn't very large, but it meant that for the first time food could be kept without spoiling. Rot and decay, the old enemies of breakfast, lunch, and dinner, were not routed, but they had suffered a significant defeat.

In those nineteenth-century kitchens, where so much work was devoted simply to *getting ready* to cook, and then to recovering from the meal and restoring the kitchen to order, nearly every family had help in the kitchen. All the household chores — cooking and cleaning and sewing and washing and ironing and mending and keeping a kitchen garden and going to market for the things you couldn't grow, plus taking care of the

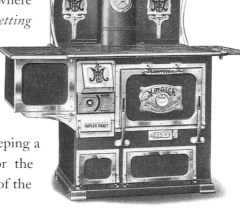

children — all this was enormously cumbersome and each activity meant hours of work. A girl in the kitchen was the norm for those who could afford her. A whole battery of servants worked in the big houses on the hill.

The Industrial Revolution changed all that. Servants left the kitchens they worked in because work in the factories paid better, the hours were shorter and more regular, and working in a factory was a step up from being a servant in someone else's house. Back in the kitchen, alone for the first time, women suddenly were faced with preparing three meals a day, and some of them didn't even know how to cook. They were saved, though, and by the same factories that had taken away their helpers, because the new factories manufactured the products — the first processed foods — that were to make

life in the kitchen easier and simpler. The gelatin that once had to be boiled for hours now came in boxes, powdered and flavored; all you had to do was add hot water and sugar and stir. Presto! Put the result in the ice box, or, soon, the electric refrigerator, and dessert was ready.

New products came tumbling out of the factories one after another. There were packages of ground tapioca and individually wrapped cakes of yeast. There was baking powder in tins. There were bottles of molasses and cans of evaporated milk. There were packages of sugar, vegetable shortening and presliced bread, bags of flour, and cooking chocolate. There were little bottles of flavoring extracts and the appearance of the almost miraculous canned foods. Canned foods, as luck would have it, were produced before there were can openers (there wasn't any point in having an opener without a can) and for a little while the best way to open a can of peaches was with a hatchet.

There were new foods too, exotic things like bananas and oranges and pineapples and avocados. There is a reason why good children found oranges in their

The
DEL MONTE FRUIT BOOK
Containing the FAVORITE FRUIT
RECIPES of AMERICA'S BEST
KNOWN COOKING AUTHORITIES

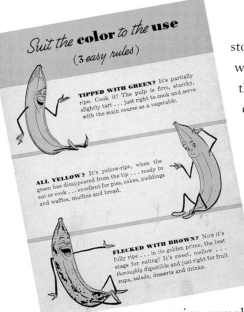

*Suit the **color** to the use*
(3 easy rules)

TIPPED WITH GREEN? It's partially ripe. Cook it! The pulp is firm, starchy, slightly tart . . . just right to cook and serve with the main course as a vegetable.

ALL YELLOW? It's yellow-ripe, when the green has disappeared from the tip . . . ready to eat or cook . . . excellent for pies, cakes, puddings and waffles, muffins and bread.

FLECKED WITH BROWN? Now it's fully ripe . . . in its golden prime, the best stage for eating! It's sweet, mellow . . . thoroughly digestible and just right for fruit cups, salads, desserts and drinks.

stockings on Christmas morning. Oranges were rare and wonderful. Santa brought them all the way from the tropics, undoubtedly cooling them at the North Pole. It was *all* awesome once — the gas stove that you turned on with little handles, the refrigerator with its art deco coil on the top, the packages with their beautiful lettering on the outside and amazing ingredients on the inside.

Women had to learn how to use these new processed and exotic foods. That was the first point of the early recipe pamphlets. Some of them focused on a single product: a pamphlet on baking cakes distributed by a flour or baking powder manufacturer like Hecker's, Rumford, or Calumet, chocolate recipes from Hershey or Baker's, gelatin desserts from Knox and Jell-O. Others were complete cookbooks, with recipes for everything, and household hints as well. Some of the all-purpose pamphlets had holes in one corner and a loop of cord threaded through the hole, presumably for hanging from a kitchen hook.

There were food adventurers behind the products and the pamphlets. They were people with vision and tenacity who took their ideas and dreams and made them real. Charles Fleischmann peddled yeast door to door and Richard Hellman figured out how to bottle his mayonnaise. Charles Knox watched his wife boil bones for gelatin and thought there must be a better way. Milton Snaveley Hershey borrowed money from his aunt so he could figure out how to coat his caramels with chocolate.

Borden's
Evaporated
Milk
Book of Recipes

The now-familiar product names belonged to real people like these and Gail Borden, James Kraft, Clarence Birdseye, and John Harvey Kellogg, among many others.

Once, we ate what we grew: rhubarb in the spring, strawberries in June, tomatoes in August, apples in the autumn, and cider in the winter. In order to have milk, you either kept a cow or you knew someone who did. Meat was pork, because pork could be preserved. When the pig was slaughtered, there was fresh meat. Other times, families ate ham and bacon, and used lard and salt pork for cooking. There were only a few foods that had to be purchased: sugar (though some families made their own sorghum and others boiled sap to make maple syrup), flour, salt, pepper, and such occasional treats as raisins and chocolate.

The food business then meant growing food, transporting it, and selling it to a hungry market. But with the onset of the Industrial Revolution and the new processed foods, the consumer suddenly had to be convinced to buy *this* kind of food rather than that, and *this* brand, not that. Before, it was a question of filling a demand. Now, a demand had to be *created*. Suddenly, the consumer had

choices. The pamphlets were part of that process, just as they were part of teaching women how to use the new foods. In a way, they led to the first liberation of women from the endless work of the kitchen.

GINGER ROGERS, co-starred in "Lucky Partners", an RKO Radio Picture.

ROYAL DESSERTS RECIPES

"A treat as thrilling as a burst of applause" says GINGER ROGERS of Royal Desserts!

The pamphlets were also part of the food trends that followed one another in succession. One of the first was for "scientific" food, food that had more to do with morality, chemistry, and a view of the rational than it did with taste. "Dainty" food looked cute and neat and helped to disassociate food on the plate from the messy reality of the kitchen. There was glamorous food, like the movie stars ate. There was food that once it was inside would keep families safe from almost any disaster — a barricade against unhappiness as well as against germs. Perhaps best of all, cooking was a way to win love — first for "Little Miss Bride" and later, for long-suffering mother.

Just after World War II, a wave of international food began, with pizza and chop suey replacing the bland innocence of chili made without chili powder or cumin or hot peppers, and curries made with a quarter teaspoon of curry powder. The tide of white sauce that had long covered our nation's plates from coast to coast began to ebb, and herbs and spices — a new world beyond salt and pepper — began to appear in lists of recipe ingredients.

Today, strawberries and asparagus are available all year around — fresh, frozen, or canned — and dozens of varieties of rice, cereal, and mustard are on supermarket shelves in cities and towns everywhere. We have freezers and microwaves, and we can zap a cup of soup, a meal, or a bowl of popcorn in mere seconds.

The old pamphlets, each one filled with its own kind of excitement and awe about its marvelous product, tell us about our past as it was reflected by food. They are a translation into food, in recipes and glowing art, of our history. Their recipes, adapted for both *The Old-Time Brand-Name Cookbook* and *Old-Time Brand-Name Desserts*, tell us what our grandparents and their parents ate for breakfast, lunch, and dinner. They are our kitchen heritage, and they still taste wonderful.

*L*eft-over pieces of plain cake or cookies may be heated carefully in a steamer, and served with sweet pudding sauce. . . .

Or they may be steamed and put into a dish covered with a boiled custard, and a meringue and served cold.

Or they may be covered with hot stewed berries or other fruit, sufficient to moisten, and served with cream.

Cakes

Or they may be used in place of bread crumbs in scalloped apple, fruit charlotte, or bread or cabinet pudding.

Stale sponge cake may be used as above, or to line a mould, or to serve as a foundation for whipped cream.

Left Overs or Economy in the Kitchen, War Edition, C. I. Hood;
Hood's Sarsaparilla, c. 1918

Banana Upside-Down Cake
(and Banana Whipped Cream Cake)

*I*n the nineteenth century, bananas were exotic fruit. Workers in the tropical fields where they grew were beset by yellow fever, malaria, and dysentery. Shippers depended on calm seas for fast voyages, and bananas were shipped only in the spring, summer, and fall, because they'd freeze aboard ship in the winter. In 1870, the Cape Cod schooner *Telegraph* picked up 160 bunches of Jamaican bananas. The captain had tried bananas and liked them and when he saw the bunches on the pier while he was loading other cargo, he decided to try bringing them back to the United States. They were still green,

and the seller told him he had 14 days before they'd spoil. The weather was good; he made it to Jersey City in two weeks, and he sold his bananas — now yellow — at a profit of $2 a bunch. The next schooner load brought bananas to Boston. Nearly 30 years later, in 1899, Boston Fruit merged with United Fruit and bananas began arriving regularly at American ports.

1 large egg

2 tablespoons melted unsalted butter plus ½ cup unsalted butter, melted (see notes)

milk

1½ cups flour

½ teaspoon baking soda (see notes)

1 teaspoon cream of tartar

1 cup sugar

½ teaspoon salt

1 teaspoon pure lemon extract

¾ cup brown sugar, loosely packed

3 bananas, peeled and sliced

1. Preheat the oven to 325 degrees.

2. Break the egg into a 1-cup measuring cup. Add the 2 tablespoons melted butter and then fill the cup with milk. Turn into a mixing bowl and beat lightly. In a separate bowl, mix together the flour, baking soda, cream of tartar, sugar, and salt. Gradually add the dry

mixture to the milk mixture, stirring to combine thoroughly. Add the lemon extract and beat until creamy.

3. Pour the remaining ½ cup melted butter into an 8-inch square baking pan. Spread the brown sugar over the bottom of the pan and then arrange the sliced bananas over the sugar. Pour the batter over the bananas.

4. Bake for 30 minutes, or until golden brown and a toothpick poked into the center of the cake comes out clean. Cool in the pan. Either turn the cake out onto a platter so that the bananas are on top, making a true upside-down cake, or make life a little easier for yourself and serve directly from the baking pan.

Notes: For this cake, butter is measured two ways: first, by spooning out 2 tablespoons of butter that has already been melted, and next by measuring ½ cup butter and *then* melting it. You can substitute 1½ teaspoons baking powder for the baking soda and cream of tartar. Finally, the cake is particularly lovely, as is almost everything, served with whipped cream.

8 to 10 servings

Adapted from "Bananas in the Modern Manner"
Banana Growers Association, 1930

Variation:
Banana Whipped Cream Cake

Make the batter for Banana Upside-Down Cake and bake it in two buttered 8-inch cake pans at 325 degrees for 30 minutes, or until golden brown and a toothpick poked into the center of the cakes comes out clean. Cool the layers on a rack. Whip 1 cup heavy cream until it's thick; sweeten with 1 tablespoon sugar and add ½ teaspoon pure vanilla extract. Place the bottom cake layer on a serving plate; cover with slices of ripe banana and spread with half the whipped cream. Place the second layer on top and heap with more bananas and the remaining whipped cream. Garnish, if you like, with a sprinkle of walnuts. Adapted from "From the Tropics to Your Table," Fruit Dispatch Company, published in 1926.

Apple Butter Refrigerator Roll

Apple Butter Refrigerator Roll sounds very fancy, but all it is at heart is a variation of the kind of dessert Girl Scouts love to make. Mind you, that doesn't diminish it one whit. Think of s'mores or Samoas or thin mint cookies: delicious then, delicious now. Teenagers often learn to cook by following an almost magical recipe for chocolate wafers sandwiched with whipped cream and left to soften into a creamy, chocolatey whole. Here, we have a grown-up variation. A favorite of mine is made with thin ginger snaps, whipped cream, and chopped crystallized ginger and the same process. At the end, I add blueberries on top. None of these recipes is adolescent. Just delectable.

1 cup heavy cream	30 vanilla wafers, the thinnest you can find
⅓ cup apple butter (see note)	chopped nuts (optional)

1. Whip the cream until it holds soft peaks. Gradually add the apple butter and continue to beat until the cream holds firm peaks.
2. Spread whipped cream mixture on one side of a wafer, top with another wafer, and spread more whipped cream on the second wafer. Stand the wafers on edge on a serving dish, and continue to add wafers and whipped cream, forming a long roll. (If your serving dish isn't large enough, make your roll two wafers wide rather than one.) When all the wafers are used, spread the remaining whipped cream mixture on the top and sides of the roll. If you like, garnish the top with chopped nuts.
3. Chill for at least 3 hours. To serve, slice diagonally across the roll.

Note: If you'd rather use another flavor of preserves, including sugar-free jam, by all means do.

6 servings

Adapted from "Recipe Book"
Heinz, 1939

Busy Mother's Cake

efore World War II, most mothers didn't have jobs outside the home. But *inside* the home, they had to boil their baby's cloth diapers, handwash the laundry and hang it on the clothesline to dry, go food shopping daily at the grocer's and the butcher's, prepare a hot lunch for the family, defrost the refrigerator monthly, and, as they say, much more. There were no supermarkets, freezers, washing machines, driers, or dishwashers. There was just Mom. And along with everything else, Mom was expected to make her own desserts. And there were no cake mixes. General Mills and Pillsbury didn't introduce their mixes, in just three flavors (or colors, if you prefer) — chocolate, gold, and white — until 1948. Duncan Hines followed in 1951 with a single mix that made a white cake if you added egg white, a yellow cake if you added a whole egg, or a chocolate cake if you added an egg and cocoa. In those days, a cake for busy mothers (the butter doesn't have to be creamed) was an enticement. It still is.

¼ cup melted unsalted butter plus butter for the pan

3 eggs

1 cup sugar

4 tablespoons water

1 teaspoon pure vanilla extract

1 cup flour

1 teaspoon baking powder

1. Preheat the oven to 325 degrees. Butter an 8-inch square baking pan, two 9-inch layer cake pans, *or* two six-muffin tins.

2. Beat the eggs in a bowl until they are slightly thickened and pale yellow. Gradually beat in the sugar. Add the water and vanilla, and mix well.

3. Mix the flour and baking powder in a separate bowl and fold this mixture into the egg batter. Fold in the melted butter.

4. Pour the batter into the buttered baking pan, layer cake pans, or muffin tins.

5. Bake for 40 minutes if you are using the square dish, 30 minutes for the layer cake pans, or 20 minutes for the muffin tins. The cake is done when a toothpick poked into the center comes out clean.

10 to 12 servings

Adapted from "Requested Recipes"
New York Daily News, 1940

Devil's Food Cake

*T*he Baker's Chocolate pamphlet that this recipe comes from tells us that chocolate is "a beneficent restorer of exhausted power," and that it's good for public speakers and "all those who give to work a portion of the time needed for sleep." And because it soothes both stomach and brain, "it is the best friend of those engaged in literary pursuits."

A literary pursuit of a poetic kind must have been involved in the naming of Devil's Food Cake. Was it so named because it's a cake so deeply chocolatey, rich, and delicious that it must be sinful? Not like Angel Food Cake, which is dry, snowy, and very pale. Angel Food Cake is what you do with leftover egg whites, and it has been around since the 1870s. Devil's Food Cake uses whole eggs, and it appeared later, just after the turn of the century. Were we more wicked then? First Paradise and then the Fall? To consider these questions, it might be wise to have a piece of devilishly good Devil's Food Cake and engage in some literary pursuits of your own.

½ cup unsalted butter at room temperature
  plus butter for the cake pans
3 squares (3 ounces) unsweetened chocolate
2 cups cake flour
1 teaspoon baking soda

2 cups sifted brown sugar, loosely packed
2 eggs
1¼ cups buttermilk
1 teaspoon pure vanilla extract

1. Butter two 8-inch cake pans.
2. Preheat the oven to 325 degrees and as the oven heats up, melt the chocolate in a dry pan, watching it carefully; it will soften in a very few minutes. Remove the pan from the oven and allow to cool slightly. In a small bowl, combine the cake flour and the baking soda. Set aside.
3. Cream the butter, and gradually add the brown sugar, continuing to beat until the mixture is light and fluffy. Add the eggs, one at a time, beating thoroughly after each. Add the chocolate, and mix well. Alternately and by thirds, add the flour mixture and the buttermilk, beginning and ending with flour and beating after each addition until smooth. Add the vanilla and mix again. Divide the batter between the buttered cake pans.
4. Bake for 35 minutes, or until a toothpick poked into the center of the cakes comes out clean.

Here we have the beginning and ending of two fables, one happy and one sad. The first "Little Bride" made her husband's birthday cake the right way: she used Gold Medal flour and a

Gold Medal recipe. And her husband loved her for it. The other husband — "poor chap" — was presented with a messy, gloppy looking cake, made with any old flour, and could barely choke down a few bites. Thus does baking become a moral force: the second marriage is obviously doomed, unless the Little Bride learns more about brand names. To me, though the second bride looks a bit more like a free spirit — her husband is her main problem. And the first marriage is just a bit too perfect. Look at their faces! You know right away you don't want to invite them over for dinner. Will they live happily ever after — just Mr. and Mrs. Perfect and their beautiful cake? Don't count on it.

Note: Frost, or serve with whipped cream or ice cream. There are some who serve a piece of cake with a scoop of ice cream and top it off with chocolate sauce. Talk about devilish!

8 to 10 servings

Adapted from "Chocolate Cookery"
Baker's Chocolate, 1929

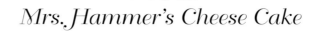

Mrs. Hammer's Cheese Cake

Cheesecake has a long and honorable pedigree. It was one of the earliest printed recipes: The Roman statesman Cato the Elder included in his writings a recipe for a ricotta cheesecake made with honey. But I'm sure cheesecake goes back even further, to the moment when someone noticed that curd cheese tasted wonderful mixed with something sweet. Smooth cheesecakes came long after Cato's noble Roman ricotta cheesecake. Best known of the smooth cheesecakes is what's known as New York cheesecake, made famous by Lindy's and made frozen by Sara Lee.

Smooth cheesecake was cooked for the first time in the last third of the nineteenth century, when cream cheese was developed in upstate New York. At first, cream cheese was made by the Empire Cheese Company. When its factory burned down, a group of farmers bought the company and reopened it as the Phenix Cheese Company, in honor of the phoenix (which they spelled wrong), the mythical bird that rose from ashes to live again. Phenix was bought by Joseph Kraft, who didn't come from upstate New York and thus named *his* product Philadelphia Cream Cheese.

But who was Mrs. Hammer? She was a woman who made good cheesecake.

2 tablespoons unsalted butter, melted, plus butter for the pan

14 slices zwieback, crushed (see note)

2 tablespoons sugar plus 1 cup

1 teaspoon cinnamon

1½ pounds pot or cottage cheese (see note)

4 eggs

1 teaspoon lemon juice

grated rind of 1 lemon

1 tablespoon flour

1 cup heavy cream, or, if using cottage cheese, ¾ cup

8 ounces crushed pineapple in its own juice, well drained (optional)

1. Preheat the oven to 350 degrees. Butter an 8-inch springform pan or an 8-inch square baking pan.
2. Crush the zwieback by pulsing in a food processor or by placing zwieback between two sheets of wax paper and crushing with a rolling pin. Mix the crumbs with 2 tablespoons

sugar, the cinnamon, and melted butter. Reserve ¼ cup of this mixture. Pat the remaining mixture over the sides and bottom of the buttered pan. Set aside.

3. If you have a food processor, combine the pot cheese with the eggs, adding them one at a time, and pulsing each into the cheese. Otherwise, in a large mixing bowl, combine the cheese with the eggs, adding them one at a time. Add the lemon juice and rind, the remaining 1 cup of sugar, and the flour, pulsing several times, or mixing well. Blend in the cream. (Be sure to use only ¾ cup of cream if you're using cottage rather than pot cheese.)

4. Scatter the pineapple, if using, over the crumbs in the baking pan. Pour in the cheese batter and sprinkle the reserved crumbs over the top.

5. Bake for 1 hour, or until firm in the center. Turn off the heat but leave the cake in the oven, with the door propped slightly open, until it is no longer hot. Then remove it and allow it to cool to room temperature. If you're using the springform pan, run a knife between the sides of the form and the cake and then remove the pan's sides. If you're using the square baking pan, serve the cake directly from the pan. Refrigerate to keep.

Note: Zwieback is a rectangular piece of bread that has been slowly toasted until it's dry and hard. You can find zwieback in the cookie section of your supermarket; if it's not there, look among the baby foods — it's a good, chewy snack for teething babies. Pot cheese is usually available in the cottage cheese section of the dairy case at your supermarket.

10 servings

Adapted from "Requested Recipes"
New York Daily News, 1940

Dutch Crumb Cake

A very refined crumb cake is this — no mile-high coating of crumbs, just a discreet topping of butter, brown sugar, and flour. It is quiet and unassuming, by nature tender and delicate, sweet, but with a slight hint of buttermilk's tang. In short, it's delectable.

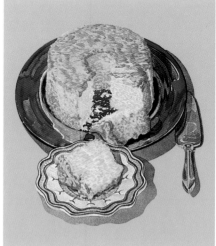

2½ cups cake flour
½ teaspoon salt
½ teaspoon baking soda
½ cup unsalted butter at room temperature
  plus butter for the pan
1½ cups brown sugar, lightly packed
1 cup raisins (optional)
1 egg, lightly beaten
¾ cup buttermilk
2 tablespoons granulated sugar
¼ teaspoon cinnamon

1. Preheat the oven to 350 degrees. Butter an 8-inch square baking pan.
2. Combine the flour, salt, and baking soda. Set aside.
3. Cream the butter thoroughly. Gradually add the brown sugar and continue beating until light and fluffy. Stir in the flour. Remove ¾ cup of this mixture and reserve it.
4. Add the raisins, if using, to the remaining butter and sugar mixture. Add the egg and buttermilk and beat well.
5. Pour the batter (which is fairly thick) into the buttered pan, levelling the top with a spatula. Sprinkle the reserved butter and flour mixture over the batter. Combine the granulated sugar and cinnamon and sprinkle on top of the butter and flour mixture.
6. Bake for 30 to 40 minutes, until lightly browned and a toothpick poked into the cake comes out clean.

10 to 12 servings

Adapted from "Home Baked Delicacies"
Swans Down, 1929

Ersatz (or Quick) Dobos Torte

Ersatz (or Quick) Dobos Torte is a wonderfully elaborate and delicious variation of pound cake. *Ersatz* is a German word meaning not the real thing; in this case, the real thing would take a whole lot longer to produce. The ersatz cake starts with an already baked pound cake.

The recipe is from a pamphlet published during the heyday of American railroads, when the Santa Fe Railway's signature train, the Super Chief, brought excellent service to the Southwest. Many of its stops were just for eating at Harvey House restaurants. When the train had a dining car, Harvey House also supplied meals on board and, let it be noted, served 1,100 pounds of this cake every year. The recipe was one of the most requested by passengers, and was published in the "Super Chief Cook Book," which notes that it is ersatz because the special baking pans needed to make a real Dobos Torte are not always available to home bakers. It's an elegant extravaganza, ersatz or otherwise.

1 pound cake, fresh or frozen
1⅓ cups semisweet chocolate chips
⅔ cup heavy cream
½ pound sweet chocolate

1. Trim the crusts from the cake. Cut the cake in half lengthwise, and slice each half into 6 or 8 very thin slices, parallel to the top.
2. Melt the chocolate chips in a double boiler over hot water; remove from the heat and let cool.
3. Whip the cream until it holds firm peaks. Fold the cooled chocolate into the whipped cream.
4. Spread the chocolate cream between the slices of each half cake, placing each slice on top of the one before.
5. Melt the sweet chocolate in a clean, dry double boiler over hot water. Cool slightly and pour over the top and sides of the cakes to make a thin coating. Chill until firm. Slice and serve.

2 cakes, or 16 servings

Adapted from "Super Chief Cook Book of Famous Fred Harvey Recipes"
Santa Fe Railway and Fred Harvey Restaurants, undated

Lady Goldenglow Second Mystery Cake

What a name! Who could resist it? This cake joins the tiny ranks of noble cakes, best known of which is Lady Baltimore Cake made with egg whites, and Lord Baltimore Cake made with yolks — something like Jack Sprat and the missus of Mother Goose fame.

Perhaps the cake is called Goldenglow because half of it is made with orange extract. And maybe the Mystery is because it's marbled: How do they do that? (It's really simple, just a spoonful of this followed by a spoonful of that.) The *Second* mystery is probably because there's a *First* Mystery Cake. It has a subtitle, Tropic Aroma Cake, but no Mystery. And it isn't noble, like Lady Goldenglow, which has it all.

1 cup unsalted butter at room temperature
  plus butter for the pan

2 cups sugar

4 eggs

3 cups flour

1 tablespoon baking powder

½ teaspoon salt

1 cup milk

1 teaspoon pure orange extract

1½ squares (1½ ounces) unsweetened
  chocolate, melted

1 teaspoon pure vanilla extract

ORANGE FROSTING:

½ cup unsalted butter

pinch of salt

grated zest of 1 orange

1 teaspoon pure orange extract

4 cups sifted confectioners' sugar

5 tablespoons milk or orange juice, as
  needed

ORANGE WHIPPED CREAM:

1½ cups heavy cream

4 tablespoons sugar

grated zest of 1 orange

1 teaspoon pure orange extract

sweet or bittersweet chocolate shavings
  or sprinkles (optional)

1. Preheat the oven to 325 degrees. Butter 2 layer-cake pans.
2. Cream the butter until it's soft and light. Gradually add the sugar, beating well and stopping to scrape down the sides of the bowl at least once. Add the eggs, one at a time, beating after each addition.
3. Mix the flour, baking powder, and salt in a separate bowl, and add to the batter in thirds, alternating with the milk,

beginning and ending with the flour mixture. Remove half the batter to a separate bowl. Add the orange extract to the batter remaining in the first bowl, and mix thoroughly. Add the melted chocolate and vanilla to the second bowl and mix well.

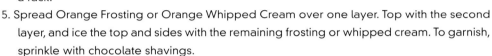

4. Divide the batter between the cake pans by tablespoons: first one of the orange mixture, then one of the chocolate, and so on. Bake for 30 to 40 minutes, or until a toothpick poked into the center of the cakes comes out clean. Cool on a rack.

5. Spread Orange Frosting or Orange Whipped Cream over one layer. Top with the second layer, and ice the top and sides with the remaining frosting or whipped cream. To garnish, sprinkle with chocolate shavings.

ORANGE FROSTING: Cream the butter with the salt, orange zest, and orange extract; gradually add the sugar and milk or orange juice, adding more milk or juice as needed to make a spreadable frosting.

ORANGE WHIPPED CREAM: Whip the cream until soft peaks form; add the sugar, grated zest, and orange extract, and beat until firm.

Note: It's also possible to use half orange and half chocolate frosting — one for the filling and one for the top. In that case, before adding the orange zest and extract to the frosting, remove half, just as you did for the cake, and add orange extract to one half and 1½ squares (1½ ounces) chocolate, melted and cooled, to the other. Use the chocolate icing as filling and the orange icing on the top and sides of the cake. You can also fill the cake with Orange Whipped Cream and ice it with Orange Frosting.

10 servings

Adapted from "Royal Cook Book"
Standard Brands, Inc., 1930

W hether one is giving an affair, or whether a friend or two drop in during the afternoon, or whether one is alone, the custom of a cup of Afternoon Tea between four and five o'clock is well worth instituting.

Make ready an afternoon tea shelf in your butler's pantry, or in a corner of your kitchen cupboard. On it assemble . . . a crystal jar filled with lemon, lime, and cinnamon drops for those who like a bit of flavor in the tea, some whole cloves for those who prefer this flavor, and one of those adorable enameled cooky boxes, which you can fill once a week with

Cookies

some old-fashioned seed cakes, hermits, or ginger drops when you do your Saturday baking . . . .

Before long you will undoubtedly find your informal Afternoon Teas growing so popular that you will wish to institute a little "At Home" every week . . . . Your simple refreshments, including the perfect tea and coffee that you will serve, and a bit of good music will soon make you famous as a hostess.

"Coffee or Tea?"
Maxwell House, undated, c. 1920

Hattie's Sugar Cookies

Cookie. The very sound of the word is sweet, playful, and innocent. *Cookie* comes from the Dutch word *koekje*, which means little cake, but there's a vast difference between a cookie and a cake. Cake is a serious thing, but cookies are pert and cute and diminutive. Cake is all grown up and well educated. Cookies are full of fun and irreverence. Cakes have icing, and layers; they get dressed up and go to weddings. Cookies stay home and eat at the children's table. The grown-ups take a cookie when they think no one is looking. Cakes are decorated, and they have decorum. Cookies are complete unto themselves and they're very easy to carry around. Hattie's Sugar Cookies are in the classic cookie mode. Like peanuts, one is too many and a thousand is not enough.

2 tablespoons unsalted butter plus butter
  for the cookie sheet
$\frac{1}{2}$ cup sugar
1 egg, lightly beaten
2 tablespoons milk
$\frac{1}{2}$ teaspoon pure vanilla extract

$\frac{2}{3}$ cup flour
1 teaspoon baking powder
pinch of salt
$\frac{1}{3}$ cup chopped pecans or walnuts
pecan or walnut halves (optional)

1. Preheat the oven to 375 degrees. Butter a cookie sheet.
2. Cream the butter. Gradually add the sugar, continuing to beat, stopping at least once to scrape down the sides of the bowl, until the mixture is light and fluffy. Add the egg and beat thoroughly. Add the milk and vanilla and combine.
3. Mix the flour, baking powder, and salt in a separate bowl, and stir this mixture into the creamed batter. Stir in the chopped nuts. Drop teaspoonfuls of batter about 2 inches apart onto the cookie sheet. If you like, press a nut half into the center of each cookie.
4. Bake for 10 to 12 minutes, until the cookies are a delicate brown with darker edges. Remove to a rack to cool.

Yield: 1 to 2 dozen cookies, depending on size

Adapted from "Home Cooking Album"
Wilkin Whiskey, 1935

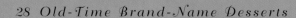

Blueberry Drop Cookies

Blueberries all year round! That's just one of the many culinary blessings we take for granted. Still, there is nothing as good as that first mouthful of fresh, local berries — unwrapped at the sink, rinsed, and eaten by the handful. The only thing better is if you've picked them yourself and gobbled a few right then and there. Blueberries are good with cream, in pancakes, in smoothies, with cereal, in pies, cakes, and — if you hadn't considered it — in cookies as well.

1/2 cup unsalted butter at room temperature plus butter for the cookie sheet

1 cup sugar

1 egg, lightly beaten

1/2 cup milk

grated rind of 1/2 lemon

2 1/2 cups flour

1/4 teaspoon salt

2 1/2 teaspoons baking powder

1 cup blueberries

1. Preheat the oven to 350 degrees. Butter a cookie sheet.

2. Cream the butter. Gradually add the sugar and mix well. Add the egg, continuing to beat.

3. In a separate bowl, combine the milk and lemon rind and, in another bowl, combine the flour, salt and baking powder. Add the milk and flour mixtures alternately to the butter, beginning and ending with the flour. Gently stir in the blueberries.

4. Drop by spoonfuls about 1/2 inch apart onto the buttered sheet. Bake for 12 to 15 minutes, or until lightly browned.

Yield: 4 to 5 dozen cookies

Adapted from "Rumford Everyday Cook Book for the Housekeeper and Student"
Rumford Baking Powder, undated, c. 1900

Brownies

Brownies are a psychological adaptation. They're a piece of chocolate cake in the relatively guilt-free guise of a cookie. They've been an American favorite since the end of the nineteenth century, predating our other national chocolate inspiration, the chocolate chip cookie.

We owe a great deal to Milton Snaveley Hershey, who encountered failure several times before he enjoyed success. In 1876, he borrowed money from his aunt to open a candy shop in Philadelphia. It failed. He opened a small caramel factory. In three years he was bankrupt. He borrowed more money and started over with more caramels, now tissue-wrapped. He almost didn't make it again, but in 1891, he decided to dip his caramels in chocolate. And in 1900, he sold his Lancaster Caramel Company for a million dollars, reserving the right to continue to sell chocolate. He had noticed that children eating his chocolate-covered caramels licked off the coating and threw away the caramels. "Caramels are a fad," he said. "I'll stake everything on chocolate." He was right. He was also right to drop his middle name. Would *you* buy a package of Snaveley's kisses?

½ cup unsalted butter at room temperature
  plus butter for the baking dish
1 cup flour
pinch of salt
1 cup sugar

2 eggs
½ teaspoon pure vanilla extract
2 squares (2 ounces) unsweetened
  chocolate, melted
½ cup chopped walnuts

1. Preheat the oven to 350 degrees. Butter an 8-inch square baking dish.
2. Mix the flour with the salt. In a separate bowl, cream the butter. Gradually add the sugar and continue to beat until light and fluffy. Add the eggs one at a time, beating after each. Beat in the vanilla and the chocolate. Gradually add the flour mixture and combine thoroughly. Stir in the walnuts. Spread the batter evenly in the buttered baking dish.
3. Bake for 40 minutes, or until a toothpick poked into the center comes out dry. (A few moist crumbs are fine, but wet batter is not.) Cut into squares and remove from the pan while still warm.

Yield: 12 to 16 brownies

Adapted from "Hershey's Recipes"
Hershey Chocolate Corporation, 1940

Blondies

Blondies are not brownies. That's the beginning of their claim to fame. While Milton Snaveley Hershey may whirl in his grave at the thought of brownies without chocolate, they are excellent nonetheless. Eating them is like discovering a secret or putting aside the obvious and getting to the heart of the matter. The not-a-brownie, better known as a blondie, is a subtle treat, like a wink between friends. I could have been a brownie, they say, but I like myself better this way. In a perfect world, where everybody has a cookie for each hand, one would be a brownie and one would be a blondie.

⅓ cup unsalted butter at room temperature plus butter for the baking dish
⅓ cup sugar
⅓ cup molasses

1 egg
1 cup flour
½ teaspoon baking powder
1 cup chopped pecans or walnuts

1. Preheat the oven to 325 degrees. Butter an 8-inch square baking dish.
2. Cream the butter and gradually add the sugar, continuing to cream, and stopping at least once to scrape down the sides of the mixing bowl. Beat in the molasses and the egg. In a separate bowl, combine the flour with the baking powder and gradually add this mixture to the batter. Beat well, and stir in the nuts. The batter will be thick. Pour or spoon it into the buttered baking dish, levelling the top with a spatula.
3. Bake for 35 minutes, or until golden brown. Cut into squares and remove from the pan while still warm.

Yield: 12 to 16 blondies

Adapted from "Cook Book"
Ceresota Flour, undated

Meringues and Variations

A meringue is just a puff of air, a wisp of sugar made crisp, an idea that melts in your mouth. Meringues are next door to magic, a zephyr of a cookie that becomes a memory even before it's gone.

There are wonderful things to be done with meringues. You can scoop out their centers and fill them with whipped cream or ice cream and berries and top them with chocolate sauce or fruit syrup, sandwich two together with jam, or add cocoa to make chocolate kisses, so gentle and sweet, though they hint at wickedness, that they are undoubtedly food for poets as well as for lovers.

And remember, they have no cholesterol. Egg whites and sugar. That's almost all they are.

4 egg whites	1 cup sugar
pinch of salt	1/2 teaspoon pure vanilla extract
1/8 teaspoon cream of tartar	

1. Preheat the oven to 300 degrees. Line a cookie sheet with parchment or waxed paper.
2. Beat the egg whites in a scrupulously clean and dry mixing bowl. As they begin to foam, add the salt and cream of tartar, and continue to beat. As they become firm, slowly and gradually add the sugar and vanilla, beating until the whites are thick and glossy and the sugar is completely dissolved.

3. Using a tablespoon or a pastry bag, form mounds of meringue on the parchment paper, about 2 inches apart. Bake until the meringues are dry and very pale brown. (To make perfectly white meringues, bake at 200 degrees for 3 hours, and let them cool in the turned-off oven.)

Variation: For cocoa meringues, beat 3 egg whites until stiff. Gradually add 1 cup sugar, beating constantly. Add 1 teaspoon pure vanilla extract and $1/2$ teaspoon vinegar and beat for 5 minutes, until stiff and glossy and the sugar is completely dissolved. Stir in $3\,1/2$ tablespoons cocoa. Drop by tablespoonfuls on a baking sheet covered with parchment or waxed paper. Bake at 275 degrees for 30 minutes, or until dry. You can eat these plain or you can add strawberries, vanilla ice cream, and chocolate whipped cream (see page 88). Yum.

Yield: 2 to 3 dozen meringues

Meringues adapted from ""Home Partners," Certified and Merit Breads, 1924
Cocoa Meringues adapted from "Hershey's Recipes," Hershey Chocolate Corporation, 1940

Orange Lunch Box Cookies

Sometime around 6600 B.C. the wheel was invented. In about 4000 B.C. oranges were cultivated. And the orange crate was hammered together for the first time by inventor E. Bean in 1875. Progress is slow, but inevitable. The crate led to the wide-scale distribution and marketing of oranges, and before too long, oranges were a lunch box staple. With good reason. They are portable, come in their own package (easily unwrapped), and are sweet, juicy, and healthful. A 1916 Sunkist pamphlet tells us that "Oranges . . . ought to be used as freely as the financial ability of the consumer may permit. A laboring man may not be able always to eat oranges at breakfast, yet the fruit is usually very cheap, and the consumption of it will obviate the need of physic and save many a doctor's bill." Put an orange in a cookie!

½ cup unsalted butter plus butter for
  the cookie sheet
1 cup sugar
2 egg yolks
grated rind of 1 orange

¼ cup orange juice
1½ cups flour
2 teaspoons baking powder
¼ teaspoon salt

VICTORY LUNCH BOXES

Never before have wives and mothers been so aware of the importance of making certain that their husbands and children are getting the kind of food which builds and maintains physical fitness and mental alertness. The failure of so many young men to pass the physical examinations for our armed forces, due to the results of faulty nourishment, has done more to stress the value of a well-balanced diet than all the teaching of years gone by.

"Victory Lunch Box Meals"
Pet Evaporated Milk, 1942

1. Cream the butter. Gradually add the sugar, continuing to beat until light and fluffy, stopping at least once to scrape down the sides of the bowl. Add the egg yolks and beat thoroughly. Mix in the orange rind and juice. In a separate bowl, combine the flour, baking powder, and salt, and fold this mixture into the batter. Wrap the dough in plastic wrap or aluminum foil and chill for several hours or overnight.

2. Preheat the oven to 375 degrees. Butter a cookie sheet.

3. Remove the dough from the refrigerator, and let it sit at room temperature for a minute or two. Roll the dough out between two sheets of lightly floured waxed paper to a thickness of ⅓ inch. Cut out circles with a biscuit cutter or the floured rim of a glass. Reroll the scraps and cut again. If the dough is too sticky, place it in the freezer for a few minutes. Place the circles at least 2 inches apart on the baking sheet — they spread as they bake.

4. Bake for 15 minutes. For a crisp cookie, bake a minute or two longer. Remove from the pan and cool on a rack. If desired, ice with Orange Frosting. (See page 24 for recipe).

Yield: 2 to 3 dozen cookies, depending on size

Adapted from "Seald Sweet Cook Book"
Florida Citrus Exchange, undated

Chocolate Bittersweet Cookies

The chocolate chip cookie story goes like this: In 1795, Amelia Simmons's *American Cookery* became the first cook book to be published in America. One of its recipes was for a lovely cookie made with both brown and white sugar.

Now it's 1933. Ruth Wakefield is baking cookies for the inn she and her husband own. Her recipe is almost exactly the same as Amelia Simmons's. But she wants to bake *chocolate* cookies, and she's in a rush. She decides that if she adds chopped chocolate pieces to the batter, the chocolate will melt in the oven and she will have saved the time involved in melting it separately. But the chocolate doesn't melt — it stays in separate pieces — and the cookies are wonderful. She names them after her Toll House Inn. Six years later, Nestlé starts distributing chocolate that is *already* chopped. The company buys the rights to the Toll House name and recipe, and packages its chocolate bits in a cellophane bag with a picture of the Toll House Inn in the corner.

And a year after *that*, Hershey publishes its pamphlet of chocolate recipes, including one for chocolate chip cookies that is almost exactly the same as the Nestlé recipe, which is almost exactly the same as the Amelia Simmons recipe, but changes its name to Chocolate Bittersweet Cookies. A cookie by any other name, Shakespeare almost said, still tastes as sweet.

In 1940, when this recipe was published, Hershey's wasn't making bittersweet bits — the recipe includes directions for breaking an eight-ounce bar of Hershey's bittersweet chocolate into little bitty pieces, and a note that if you would rather have milk chocolate cookies, you can simply chop up a large bar of Hershey's milk chocolate to use instead.

1 cup flour
1 teaspoon baking powder
1/8 teaspoon salt
1/2 cup unsalted butter, at room temperature
1/2 cup brown sugar, packed
1/4 cup granulated (white) sugar
1 egg
1/2 teaspoon pure vanilla extract
1/3 cup walnut pieces
8 ounces semi-sweet chocolate bits

1. Preheat the oven to 350 degrees.
2. Mix the flour, baking powder, and salt in a small bowl.
3. Cream the butter with the two sugars until it is light and fluffy. Beat in the egg and vanilla.
4. Gradually beat the flour mixture into the butter mixture. Add the nuts and the chocolate and combine thoroughly.
5. Drop by rounded tablespoonfuls onto an ungreased cookie sheet.
6. Bake for 10 minutes, or until golden brown. Let stand on the sheet for 2 to 3 minutes before transferring to wire racks to cool.

Yield: 2 dozen cookies

Adapted from "Hershey's Recipes"
Hershey Chocolate Corporation, 1940

Reprinted from *The Old-Time Brand-Name Cookbook,* by Bunny Crumpacker
Smithmark Publishers, 1998

Chocolate Pinwheels

These are cookies that are fun for children to make, and they're certainly fun for children to eat. The pinwheel effect is pretty, though it verges on fuss for the sake of fuss. I imagine these cookies were popular at old-fashioned tea parties. The thing is that they don't have to be perfect; I think they're even nicer when the pinwheel effect is a little lopsided and splotchy; they look a little more homemade that way. Isn't that a happy thought? Of course, there's nothing wrong with perfection. They're good either way. And a happy reward for patient children.

1½ cups flour
1 teaspoon baking powder
pinch of salt
½ cup unsalted butter at room
  temperature

½ cup sugar
1 egg yolk, lightly beaten
3 tablespoons milk
1 square (1 ounce) unsweetened
  chocolate, melted

The nervousness and peevishness of our times are chiefly attributable to tea and coffee; the digestive organs of confirmed coffee drinkers are in a state of chronic derangement, which reacts upon the brain, producing fretful and lachrymose moods. Cocoa and chocolate are neutral in their physical effects, and are really the most harmless of our fashionable drinks.

Dr. Karl Ernest "Cocoa and Chocolate"
Walter Baker & Company, Ltd., 1917

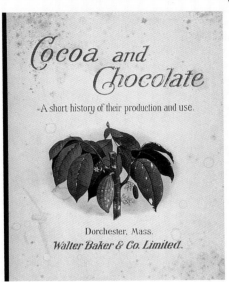

1. Mix the flour, baking powder, and salt. In a separate bowl, cream the butter and gradually add the sugar. When the mixture is light, add the egg yolk and mix well. Alternately add the flour mixture and milk, and mix until smooth. Divide the batter in half. Add the melted chocolate to one half; and refrigerate the chocolate half while you work with the plain.

2. Place the plain batter on a lightly floured sheet of waxed paper and, using a floured rolling pin, roll it into an ⅛-inch-thick rectangle. Roll up, with the waxed paper, from the narrow edge, and refrigerate while you work with the chocolate batter.

3. Repeat the rolling-out process with the chocolate batter. Leave it in place and unroll the plain batter, placing it over the chocolate sheet and removing the waxed paper. Roll the two layers up together, from the narrow edge, like a jelly roll. Cover with plastic wrap, and refrigerate for at least 12 hours.

4. Preheat the oven to 425 degrees.

5. Unwrap the roll, and cut it into ⅛-inch-thick cookies. Place on an ungreased cookie sheet and bake for 10 minutes. The white part of the cookies may brown slightly; this won't affect the taste, but if you'd rather have the chocolate-vanilla look, lower the heat slightly and watch carefully as the cookies bake.

Yield: 3 dozen cookies

Adapted from "Best Chocolate Recipes"
Walter Baker & Company, Inc., 1932

How to Save Time

When a "job" is done, forget it. Thinking about it is like doing it twice.

Keep the ice-box cleared out and clean it daily.

Make enough pie crust at one time for several pies.

Teach the family to pick up their bed rooms while they dress.

What You Can Do with the Time You Save

Attend the Woman's Club, the Woman's Church Society, Sewing Club, Parent-Teacher Association, some Lodge, the Grange, etc.

Take up again your music, languages, dancing.

Pies

Make dainty accessories for yourself or your house.

Serve informal afternoon tea once or twice a month — indoors in cold weather — on the piazza or outdoors in warm weather.

Do a little gardening.

Read some new books — outdoors in suitable weather.

Visit the shops occasionally.

From "Home Partners" by Ida Bailey Allen
Certified and Merit Breads, 1924

Sour Cream Apple Pie

The power of apples is amply demonstrated by the contretemps in the Garden in Eden and also in the word itself. As the fruit spread throughout northern Europe from its Indo-European roots, the word *abel* went with it: In German, apple is *apfel;* in Dutch, *appel;* in Russian, *jabloko;* in English, *apple.* The Latin word for fruit, *pomum,* became the French *pomme* for apple. The French must have thought apples were an outstanding example of fruit. All these words testify to the enormous gift of apples. From blossom to fruit, they delight the eye and please the palate. We like to think that apple pie is the quintessential American dessert, but in fact, there are ample references to apple pies all the way back to the Middle Ages, long before Columbus set sail. Perhaps that's one reason why apple pie is the perfect American dessert. With its heritage from many cultures and peoples, it is a dessert with ethnic variations. This one (based in part on a recipe from *The New York Times Menu Cookbook*) is rich with sour cream, and ranks with the very best.

1 unbaked 9-inch pie crust
2 eggs, lightly beaten
½ cup sugar plus ⅓ cup
2 tablespoons flour plus 2 additional
   tablespoons
pinch of salt
1 cup sour cream (regular or ⅓ less fat,
   not fat free)

4 tart apples (such as Granny Smiths),
   peeled, cored, and sliced
¼ teaspoon nutmeg, freshly grated
   if possible
3 tablespoons unsalted butter

1. Preheat the oven to 350 degrees. Line a 9-inch pie pan with the unbaked crust.
2. Combine the eggs, ½ cup sugar, 2 tablespoons flour, the salt, and sour cream in a mixing bowl, and add the apples, mixing well. Pour into the pie crust and bake for 10 minutes.
3. While the pie is baking, combine the remaining flour and sugar in a mixing bowl or a food processor bowl. Add the nutmeg and, using a pastry cutter, two knives, or the processor, cut in the butter until the mixture is crumbly. Sprinkle it over the apples and bake for 30 minutes longer, or until the crumbs are brown and the apples are tender.

8 servings

Adapted from "Sour Cream Recipes"
Milk Industry Foundation, undated

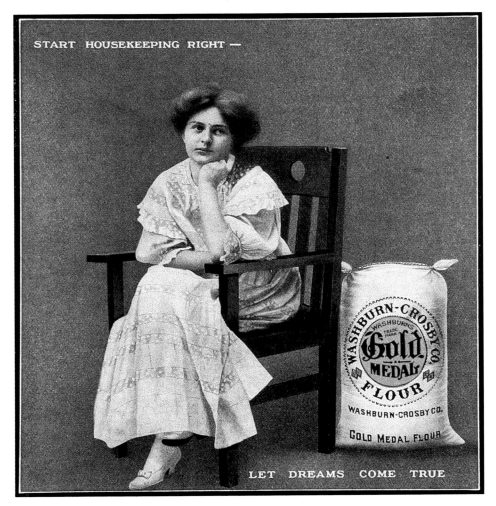

Jam Turnovers

What's special about these flexible treats is their cream cheese crust. It's easy, but it's respectable — you'll still think well of it in the morning. It's remarkably easy to handle. You can prepare it today, and bake it tomorrow; you can freeze it and use it next week; you can use it for a sweet little one-bite baby pie, or for a savory quiche or tart. It doesn't need fussing. It forgives your sins. Of course, it *is* rich. But we're talking pie crust here, not broccoli. You could fill it with broccoli and let the good guys and the bad guys fight it out once they get inside you. Or you could have broccoli for dinner and Jam Turnovers for dessert. That's what I would do.

1 cup unsalted butter (two sticks) at room temperature

8 ounces cream cheese at room temperature (use regular cream cheese, *not* whipped or low fat)

2 cups flour plus flour for rolling out the dough

2 tablespoons sugar

¼ cup jam or jelly (regular or unsweetened)

1. Cream the butter and cream cheese in a mixing bowl until they are well blended. Add the flour and sugar and mix just until the dough holds together. Form it into a roll about two inches in diameter; cover with plastic wrap and refrigerate for at least 2 hours.

2. Preheat the oven to 400 degrees.

3. Remove the roll from the refrigerator. Turn it out onto a floured surface. Cut crosswise into ½-inch-thick slices. Roll out each slice, using a floured rolling pin, to a thickness of about ⅛-inch. Use a biscuit cutter or the floured rim of a glass to cut each slice into a circle. (The size of the circles is up to you — small ones for just a bite; larger ones for more substantial munching.) Reroll the scraps and cut again. Use only as much flour on the surface and the rolling pin as you need; too much will toughen the pastry.

BAG PAPER TEST FOR OVEN TEMPERATURE:

Place a piece of bag paper on the center
rack of the heated oven.
Count sixty.
If the paper is burnt on the edges,
the oven is "hot" or "quick."
If the paper is lightly and evenly
browned, it is "medium."
If the paper is scarcely colored, it is "cool" or "slow."
This test is helpful in determining the temperature
of the oven, but of course, it is not accurate.

"Good Pies"
Nonesuch Mincemeat, undated

4. Place a dollop of jam — about ½ teaspoon for 2-inch circles — just off center in the middle of each circle. Moisten the tip of your finger with water (fill a cup with water and leave it to one side for finger-dipping) and wet the edge of half of each circle. Fold the other half over onto the moistened edge and press to seal. Use the floured tines of a fork to press around each crescent, making a pattern of indentations and also making the seal tighter. Make a small slit in the center of each turnover or prick each one with a fork.
5. Place the turnovers on a baking sheet. Bake for 15 to 20 minutes, until golden.

Note: To use the crust for a savory filling, omit the sugar. Mushrooms sautéed with minced onion and garlic and a bit of dill or thyme make a lovely savory bite. But for this recipe, remember that much depends on the quality of the jam.

Yield: two dozen 2-inch circle turnovers

Adapted from "Famous Dishes"
Frigidaire, 1936

Blueberry Pie

*T*here isn't much in the way of blue food, but blueberries more than make up for the gap. They are lusciously, deliciously, marvelously, intensely *blue*. And when you eat them, your tongue is blue, your teeth are blue — your mouth, your whole being, is blue. Not sad blue. Happy blue. And blueberry pie is one of the happiest of blues.

4 cups blueberries, fresh or frozen
1/4 to 1/2 cup sugar, depending on the
   sweetness of the berries
pinch of salt
1/4 cup water
3 tablespoons quick-cooking tapioca

1/2 teaspoon nutmeg, freshly grated
   if possible
unbaked pastry for a 9-inch 2-crust pie
optional glaze: 1 egg, beaten with
   1 tablespoon water; or milk

1. Preheat the oven to 425 degrees.
2. Combine the blueberries and 1/4 cup sugar (taste to see if more sugar is needed); add the salt, water, tapioca, and nutmeg, and mix.
3. Line a 9-inch pie pan with the bottom crust and fill with the berries. Fit the top crust over the filling; fold the edge under the bottom crust and pinch together to seal, raising the rim all around. Crimp the edges by pinching between your thumb and the knuckle of your second finger, or press the edges with the tines of a fork. Cut a tiny hole in the middle of the crust and make several short slits around the hole. Glaze the top crust by brushing it with the egg and water mixture, or simply by brushing with milk.
4. Bake for 15 minutes; lower the heat to 350 degrees and bake for 20 minutes longer, or until the crust is golden brown.

6 to 8 servings

Adapted from "A Cook's Tour"
Minute Tapioca, 1929

Art Linkletter's Peach Pie

*A*rt Linkletter had a long and varied career on radio and television, and was probably best known for his programs featuring children who said "the darndest things." He began in broadcasting by directing radio shows from the Los Angeles Exposition, the Texas Centennial, and the San Francisco Fair, the pamphlet tells us, and goes on to add that in 1945, he was one of the top six handball players in the country. Playing handball burns off a lot of calories, and his Peach Pie is a lovely way to supply the fuel.

¾ to 1 cup sugar, depending on the sweetness of the peaches

2 tablespoons flour

¼ teaspoon salt

½ teaspoon nutmeg, freshly grated if possible

8 medium to large peaches, peeled and sliced, or 1 bag (1¼ pounds) frozen peaches

unbaked pastry for a 9-inch 2-crust pie

optional glaze: 1 egg mixed with 1 tablespoon water; or milk

1. Preheat the oven to 425 degrees.
2. Combine ¾ cup sugar, the flour, salt, and nutmeg in a mixing bowl. Mix in the peaches, and taste to see if more sugar is needed.
3. Line a 9-inch pie pan with the bottom crust and fill with the peaches. Fit the top crust over the filling; fold the edge under the bottom crust and pinch together to seal, raising the rim all around. Crimp the edges by pinching between your thumb and the knuckle of your second finger, or press the edges with the tines of a fork. Cut a tiny hole in the middle of the crust and cut several short slits around the hole. Glaze the top crust by brushing it with the egg mixture, or simply by brushing with milk.
4. Bake for 5 minutes; then lower the heat to 350 degrees and bake for 35 minutes longer, or until the crust is golden brown.

Note: The pie can be baked without the top crust; for a single-crust pie, bake until the peaches begin to bubble and brown. To peel peaches, dip them into boiling water for 15 seconds; remove them, and immediately plunge them into very cold water.

6 to 8 servings

Adapted from "Cook Book of the Stars"
WFBL, Columbia Broadcasting System Network, 1945

Trauben Kuchen (Grape Pie)

*T*here isn't really a line between cake and pie, there's more of a gulf. But *kuchen* (German for cake) crosses the nonexistent line, and falls into the gulf — or at least this *kuchen* does. It's a pie crust filled with grapes, which means it's really a pie and not a cake in any language. But in the *New York Herald Tribune*'s 1940 publication of "Prize Winning Recipes," this is called a *kuchen*. Of course, the *New York Herald Tribune* doesn't exist any more. How could anyone trust a newspaper that didn't know the difference between a cake and a pie? On the other hand, this is a prize-winning recipe. I suspect that it was someone's old family recipe, and that originally, in Germany, it was made with a *kuchen* batter bottom rather than with a pie crust. It's good this way, and it would be good that way, too.

1 unbaked 9-inch pie crust
$\frac{1}{4}$ cup sugar plus an
   additional $\frac{1}{2}$ cup
3 cups seedless grapes
1 tablespoon cornstarch
1 cup half-and-half
3 eggs, lightly beaten
$\frac{1}{2}$ teaspoon cinnamon

1. Preheat the oven to 425 degrees.
2. Line a 9-inch pie pan with the unbaked crust. Sprinkle $\frac{1}{4}$ cup sugar evenly over the crust. Place the grapes over the sugar.
3. Combine the remaining $\frac{1}{2}$ cup sugar with the cornstarch in a mixing bowl. Gradually add the half-and-half and mix until smooth. Add the eggs and mix thoroughly. Pour this mixture over the grapes, and sprinkle the top with the cinnamon.
4. Bake for 15 minutes; lower the heat to 350 degrees and bake for 30 minutes longer, or until the filling is firm. Serve cold.

6 to 8 servings

Adapted from "Prize Winning Recipes"
New York Herald Tribune, 1940

Jamaican Pumpkin Pie

Ginger was part of the ancient silk trade between China and Europe. Ginger, cinnamon, and silk went one way, and gold and silver, among other things, went the other. It was the first Asian spice to be successfully grown in the Americas— on the island of Jamaica in the Caribbean. Columbus bumped into Jamaica — we like to say he discovered it, but actually, it was there before he arrived in 1494.

Ginger is now a universal spice, used in everything from English gingerbread to Japanese pickled ginger, and with good reason. It not only tastes good, it's good for you as well, aiding digestion and warding off motion sickness. Emphasizing it in pumpkin pie is an inspired idea. Ginger marmalade is on the jam shelf of your supermarket. (If it's not, it should be, so ask.) Try the marmalade on cream cheese or yogurt on an English muffin. And enjoy it in your pumpkin pie.

1½ cups cooked pumpkin
  (fresh or canned), puréed
¼ cup brown sugar, firmly packed
1 teaspoon cinnamon
½ teaspoon salt

2 eggs, lightly beaten
1½ cups milk
½ cup heavy cream
½ cup ginger marmalade
1 unbaked 9-inch pie crust

1. Preheat the oven to 425 degrees.
2. Combine the pumpkin with the brown sugar, cinnamon, salt, and eggs in a mixing bowl. Whisk in the milk and cream, and then the ginger marmalade.
3. Line a 9-inch pie pan with the crust and pour in the pumpkin mixture. Bake for 10 minutes; lower the heat to 325 degrees and bake 40 minutes longer, or until set. A knife inserted into the pie about 1 inch from the edge will come out clean; in the middle, the custard will be almost firm. The pie will continue to cook after it's removed from the oven, so take care not to overbake it. Cool on a rack, and then chill.

Note: It's fine to substitute low-fat or skim milk for the milk and cream. The pie won't be as rich, but it will still have an excellent taste.

6 to 8 servings
Adapted from "Secrets of the Jam Cupboard"
Certo, 1932

Lemon Pie Unique

There's a reason why Sunkist, in its 1939 pamphlet, called this pie "unique." In no way is this your run-of-the-mill lemon meringue pie. Most obviously, there's no meringue. But just as clearly, there's no creamy lemon pudding under the missing meringue. What we have instead are sliced lemons — yes! sliced lemons! — tangy and bright yellow circles of pure lemon, sugary and rich. If you like lemons — *really* like lemons — you'll love this pie. It's *very* lemony. The pie may remind you of lemon bars, or lemon curd, or lemon meringue, but this is the real thing, the lemon McCoy. It's very rich, so serve it in small slices. (You can always have two.) Is it good with vanilla ice cream? Is there a pie in this wonderful world that isn't good with vanilla ice cream?

1 unbaked 8-inch pie crust
1½ cups sugar
¾ cup flour
1 teaspoon grated lemon zest

2 lemons
1 cup cold water
1 tablespoon unsalted butter

1. Preheat the oven to 425 degrees.
2. Line an 8-inch pie pan with the crust. Grate one of the lemons until you have 1 teaspoon of grated zest. In a mixing bowl, combine the sugar, flour, and lemon zest. Sprinkle 1½ cups of this mixture over the crust.
3. Peel both lemons, removing all the white pith. Cut the lemons into very thin slices, removing the seeds as you go. Place the lemons in the crust, either arranging them in careful circles, or simply piling the lemons in and levelling the top.
4. Sprinkle the remaining sugar mixture over the lemons. Pour the water over the lemons (use less water if it threatens to overflow); stir very gently (without disturbing the lemon slices if you've arranged them in circles) and dot with the butter.
5. Bake for 10 minutes; lower the heat to 325 degrees and bake for 40 to 50 minutes longer, until the lemons are lightly browned. Serve warm.

6 to 8 servings

Adapted from "Sunkist Lemons"
Sunkist, 1939

Two Sweet Potato Pies

I feel strongly about sweet potato pie. First of all, we don't eat it often enough. Secondly, we consider it an example of Southern cooking (which it is) rather than a national treasure (which it also is). Thirdly, we usually smother it in too many spices, just as we do pumpkin pie, so that the special taste of the sweet potato is lost in a mist of cinnamon and nutmeg and cloves.

Sweet potato pie is a beautiful color, it's full of vitamin A, and it's naturally sweet. This is a sweet potato pie with an unusual variation. Just don't use canned sweet potatoes. Don't even think about it.

2 cups boiled sweet potatoes, (about 3 large) mashed
2 cups milk
3 eggs, lightly beaten
1½ cups sugar

¼ teaspoon salt
1 teaspoon pure lemon or vanilla extract
pinch of nutmeg, freshly grated if possible
1 unbaked 9-inch pie crust

1. Preheat the oven to 375 degrees.
2. Combine the sweet potatoes with the milk, eggs, sugar, salt, lemon or vanilla extract, and nutmeg in a mixing bowl. Mix well.
3. Line a 9-inch pie pan with the unbaked crust, and pour in the sweet potato filling.
4. Bake for 40 to 50 minutes, until a clean, dry knife inserted an inch from the edge comes out clean. Don't overbake: The middle won't be set, but it will continue to cook after the pie is removed from the oven.

6 to 8 servings

Adapted from "Royal Cook Book"
Standard Brands Inc., 1930

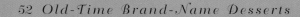

Variation: In 1910, Gold Medal Flour published a pamphlet which included this recipe for "A Different Sweet Potato Pie:" Boil 3 large sweet potatoes for 20 minutes; cool, peel, and cut into thick slices. Line a deep-dish pie pan with an unbaked crust. Arrange the sliced potatoes in layers, sprinkling each layer with sugar, cinnamon, and nutmeg (in all, use about ½ cup sugar and ½ teaspoon each of cinnamon and nutmeg). Pour 3 tablespoons whiskey, rum, or Cognac over the sweet potatoes, and follow with ½ cup water. Bake as is, or cover with a top crust, cutting a few slits in the top for steam to escape. Bake at 350 degrees for 40 minutes, or until the top crust is golden. Serve warm.

CREAM — CREAM — CREAM! You can't serve your family or guests too much . . . . for everyone loves our delicious, fresh, thick cream on fruits, cereals, soups, salads, desserts! Keep a sufficient supply in the refrigerator. Order now!

"The Sealtest Food Adviser"
Sheffield Farms, 1939

Puddings and Frozen Desserts

There seems to be a rather general feeling that desserts frozen in the electric refrigerator are expensive luxuries. As a matter of fact, the careful analysis of a collection of tested recipes shows that on the whole the cost of desserts frozen at home in the electric refrigerator is unexpectedly low.

"Cooking with Cold"
Kelvinator, 1933

Bread Pudding

read pudding is a model of what a pudding ought to be, sweet and soft, solid and sturdy, not insubstantial but not heavy either. It is a poetic and philosophic dish that nourishes and delights. Of all the puddings, bread pudding is perhaps the most practical and the most ethereal. It is practical because it uses what's left of the daily loaf, and ethereal because it turns that hearty loaf into a custardy sweetness, reminiscent of the dairy as well as the hearth. There are bread puddings with raspberries embedded in their middles like rubies. There are bread puddings served with elaborate sauces and designs. And there are bread puddings that are no more than bread, eggs, milk, and sugar, with perhaps a bit of vanilla. They are all works of wonder. Bread pudding is the sweet staff of life.

2 tablespoons melted unsalted butter plus
  butter for the baking dish
2 to 3 cups dry bread, cubed (see note)
2 cups milk
1/4 cup sugar

2 eggs, lightly beaten
1/2 teaspoon pure vanilla extract
1/4 teaspoon salt
1/2 teaspoon *each* cinnamon and nutmeg
  or 1 tablespoon brown sugar

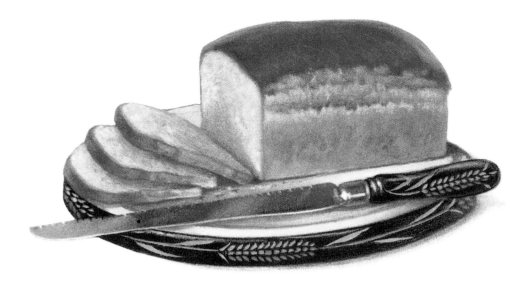

1. Preheat the oven to 350 degrees. Butter an 8-inch square baking dish.
2. Arrange the bread cubes evenly in the baking dish. Add the milk, butter, sugar, eggs, vanilla, and salt. Stir gently until all the bread is moistened. Let stand for 10 minutes and stir again. If you are using the spices, add them now and stir them in gently.
3. Bake for 45 minutes to 1 hour, until the top is browned. If you are using the brown sugar, sprinkle it evenly over the top of the pudding and set it under the broiler until it bubbles and melts. Watch carefully to prevent burning.

Note: Use the best possible bread — a homemade or bakery loaf, or substantial packaged bread like Pepperidge Farm or Arnold. Everything depends on the quality of your ingredients.

6 servings

Adapted from "Be an Artist at the Gas Range"
The Mystery Chef and Your Gas Company, 1935

Marshmallow Delight

What is a marshmallow? A playful puff, a wisp, a softness of sugar and air, a charred but sweet nibble on a stick after the scary story around the campfire. But once, marshmallows were more serious. They were made with the gummy extract of the root of the mallow plant, a perennial that grows in swamps and marshes. Yuk. Packaged and formed with gelatin instead of mallow root, they were all the rage in the 1920s and '30s. Marshmallow Fluff came along (remember Fluffer-Nutter sandwiches?) in the early 1920s, developed by a fellow with the felicitous name of Archibald Query. After some years of peddling his goo door-to-door, Mr. Query sold his sticky formula for $500 to the Durkee-Mower Company, which owns it still.

1 20-ounce can crushed pineapple,
   canned in its own juice, drained
2 cups marshmallows (either large
   and quartered, or small)
1 cup heavy cream

1. Combine the drained pineapple and the marshmallows in a mixing bowl and refrigerate for several hours. Just before serving, whip the cream and fold it in.

Note: If the pudding is too sweet, add a few drops of lemon juice. The pamphlet suggests serving with sponge cake. Why not? But it's good plain.

6 servings

Adapted from
"Hawaiian Pineapple
as 100 Good Cooks
Serve It"
Dole Pineapple, 1927

Pasha op Paska (A Russian Easter Dish)

ashka means Easter in Russian, and Pashka, or Pasha as this pamphlet calls it, is the traditional Russian Easter dessert. It is a kind of cheesecake, unbaked and made sublime with butter, sour cream, and cream or cottage cheese. In Russia, the dessert is poured into a pyramid-shaped mold with holes for drainage. When it's ready, it's decorated with almonds and candied fruits and taken to the church to be blessed by the priest. It is traditionally eaten with sweet bread, and it's wonderful that way (try panettone, brioche, or challah). It is also marvelous with fresh berries, a sweet berry sauce, or sliced peaches. When you get right down to it, it's divine spread on toasted pound cake — or just plain toast. Or go straight to heaven and just eat it with a spoon.

12 ounces cream cheese at room temperature
½ cup unsalted butter at room temperature
½ cup sour cream
½ cup sugar
Optional: any or all — ¾ cup candied orange peel, ⅓ cup dried currants, 1 cup sliced or chopped almonds

1. Mix all the ingredients together. Line a colander with two layers of rinsed and squeezed out cheesecloth, and fill with the cheese mixture. Cover with more rinsed and squeezed cheesecloth. Place a small dish over the top and a weight on top of the dish, a large can of tomatoes, for instance, or some heavy stones. Place the colander over a bowl to drain. Place in the refrigerator for at least 12 hours. Unmold, removing the cheesecloth. Serve plain, or with sweet or sour cream, or fresh or cooked fruit.

8 to 12 servings

Adapted from "Around the World Cook Book"
Kalamazoo Stoves, 1950

Three Rice Puddings

Because you can't have too much of a good thing, here are three recipes, count 'em, three, for rice pudding.

A thought about origins and etymologies: rice came west from Asia, where it was first cultivated about 5,500 years ago. A lot of rice words sound the same: in Greek *oruza*, Latin *oryza*, Russian *ris*, German *reis*, Dutch *rijst*, Danish and Swedish *ris*, Italian *riso*, Spanish *aroz*, French *riz*, and English *rice*, probably all from the Sanskrit *vrihi*, or the Afghan *vrize*. Like those words, the puddings made from rice go around the world like a theme with variations. Once, rice was expensive and rare outside Asia. It was treated like a spice rather than a basic food. But when it advanced onto the menu, it was first in the form of rice pudding. These three recipes, beginning with the most traditional, are delectable reasons for putting pudding first.

Creamy Rice Pudding

½ cup sugar	½ cup rice
½ teaspoon salt	butter for the baking dish
5 cups milk	1 teaspoon pure vanilla extract

1. Mix the sugar, salt, and 4 cups of the milk in the top of a double boiler. Heat over hot water in the lower pan and bring to the scalding point, when small bubbles form around the edge of the pan. Gradually add the rice, stirring constantly. Cover and simmer slowly until the rice is tender, about 2 hours.

2. Heat the oven to 375 degrees and butter an 8-inch square baking dish. Add the remaining cup of milk and the vanilla to the rice, stir well, and transfer to the buttered dish. Bake for 20 to 30 minutes, or until a light brown crust has formed.

6 servings

Adapted from "Be an Artist at the Gas Range"
The Mystery Chef and Your Gas Company, 1935

Chocolate Rice Pudding

1 cup milk
1 cup cooked rice
4 tablespoons cocoa
½ cup sugar

pinch of salt
½ teaspoon pure vanilla extract
cream for serving

1. Mix the milk, rice, cocoa, sugar, and salt in the top of a double boiler. Heat over hot water in the lower pan and cook until thick. Cool slightly, add the vanilla and stir. Serve with cream.

4 to 6 servings

Adapted from "Rice — 200 Delightful Ways to Serve It"
Southern Rice Industry, 1935

Hawaiian Cream Pudding

½ cup rice
2 cups milk
¼ cup sugar
pinch of salt

1 cup crushed pineapple,
   canned in its own juice,
   well drained
1 teaspoon pure vanilla extract
1 cup heavy cream

1. Mix the rice, milk, sugar, and salt in the top of a double boiler. Heat over hot water in the lower pan. Cook until the rice is tender, 1½ to 2 hours. Cool. Add the pineapple and vanilla and stir. Whip the cream, and fold it into the rice mixture. Chill.

4 to 6 servings

Adapted from "The Everyday Cook Book for the Housekeeper and Student" Rumford Baking Powder, undated

Clean-Up Week: Won't you please search your cellar for empty milk bottles and return them? We will appreciate your cooperation.

"A Year of Recipes"
Abbott's Dairies, 1933

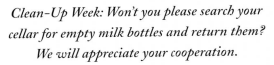

Chocolate Bavarian Cream

Bavaria is in southern Germany, but doesn't seem to have much to do with Bavarian cream, a light and fluffy creation whose roots are French — it was originally a crème bavaroise. Bavarian creams are usually made with gelatin in a custard base, lightened with beaten egg whites and whipped cream, and flavored with fruit or vanilla. This one is much simpler, but does not suffer at all for its innocence. Its heart and soul are chocolate and whipped cream. Not bad for the anatomy of a dessert!

1 tablespoon unflavored gelatin	⅓ cup sugar
¼ cup cold water	2 cups heavy cream
½ cup milk	1 teaspoon pure vanilla
2 squares (2 ounces)	extract
unsweetened chocolate	pinch of salt

1. Sprinkle the gelatin over the cold water in a small cup. Allow to stand for 5 minutes, or until the grains are softened and swollen.
2. In a small saucepan, add the chocolate to the milk and place over low heat. Stir occasionally, until the chocolate has melted. Add the gelatin and whisk until it is completely dissolved. Add the sugar, continuing to stir until it too has dissolved.
3. Set the saucepan over a bowl of cold water and let it sit, stirring occasionally, until it begins to thicken.
4. Meanwhile, whip the cream until stiff. Add the vanilla and salt. Fold the chocolate mixture into the whipped cream.
5. Moisten a mold or serving bowl by running it under cold water. Turn it over so the excess water drips out, but let it stay wet. Pour the chocolate cream into the wet mold. Refrigerate for 3 to 4 hours, or until the cream is firm.

Note: The pudding is also good soft, after only a brief chilling period; it's just different, more like a sauce than a pudding. For a frozen dessert on a hot day, put the bowl in the freezer instead of the refrigerator. Let it soften in the refrigerator for 10 minutes or so before serving.

6 servings

Adapted from "Desserts, Salads, Candies, and Frozen Dishes"
Knox Gelatin, 1933

Lemon Ice

What is the difference between ices and sherbets and sorbets and ice cream? You could say it is a matter of complications. Ices are just fruit, sugar, and water. Ice cream gets more involved, with a cream or custard base. Sherbet is in the middle. Sorbet is just the French word for sherbet.

The making of iced desserts goes way back. Marco Polo wrote of ice in China that was brought down from the mountains and scraped and flavored with fruits. Aztecs may have poured chocolate into snow, just as some old New England cookbooks have recipes for newly fallen snow mixed with cream and vanilla extract. In a world where some brave soul tasted oysters for the first time and somebody else discovered cheese, mixing snow or scraped ice with fruit flavoring must have required much less courage, and probably happened in many places with many variations.

In our day and age, ices are the perfect low-fat dessert. (Unless you serve cookies with them.) And lemon ice, a perennial favorite, is best of all.

3 cups water

1 cup sugar

½ cup freshly squeezed lemon juice

1. Place the water and sugar in a medium saucepan without stirring; bring to a boil, lower the heat, and simmer for 5 minutes.
2. Stir in the lemon juice. Cool. Strain into a bowl and place in the freezer.
3. When the mixture begins to freeze around the edges, mix it well with a fork or a whisk to prevent crystals from forming. Continue to freeze for several hours or until firm.
4. Before serving, let stand for about 10 minutes at room temperature in order to soften slightly.

Note: To make Orange Ice, use orange juice instead of lemon. A bit of grated zest can be added to either of the ices.

6 to 8 servings

Adapted from "Sunkist Recipes"
California Fruit Growers Exchange, 1916

Russian Coffee Frappé

*I*t's 1907, and Teddy Roosevelt is having a cup of coffee at a hotel in Nashville, Tennessee. The coffee he's drinking is a blend developed in the 1880s by a local resident. "Ah!" says Teddy, as he drains his cup, "Good to the last drop!" The hotel is the Maxwell House, and it is famous for its coffee. (For the record, Caleb Chase and James Sanborn — anybody remember Chase and Sanborn? — were the first to put ground coffee in sealed tin cans, in 1878.)

According to some, Russian coffee is half coffee and half cocoa. We call this mocha, and it is delicious. So is this frozen version of coffee, cocoa, and whipped cream. It's creamy and good and surprisingly refreshing.

2 cups hot, freshly brewed coffee
1 cup sugar
2 cups freshly made cocoa (see note)
pinch of salt

1 cup heavy cream
1 teaspoon pure vanilla extract
cinnamon

1. Pour the hot coffee over the sugar in a heatproof bowl or saucepan and stir until the sugar is dissolved. Add the cocoa and the salt and stir. Cool.

2. Whip the cream until it's thick, and stir in the vanilla. Fold the cream into the coffee mixture until thoroughly blended. Pour into a mold or serving bowl and place in the freezer for 3 hours, or until frozen. Dust the top lightly with cinnamon. Soften in the refrigerator for 10 to 15 minutes before serving.

Note: To make the cocoa, mix 2 heaping teaspoons cocoa and 4 teaspoons sugar in a heatproof cup (a large Pyrex measuring cup works well) or a small saucepan. Stir in a teaspoon or two of milk or cream to make a thick paste and then add hot milk, cream, or water (or a mixture) to make 2 cups.

8 servings

Adapted from "Coffee or Tea?"
Maxwell House Coffee, undated, c. 1925

SECRETS

of Coffee Flavor
and some Unusual Recipes

Vienna Coffee

*T*his sweetly simple recipe is adapted from a pamphlet published in 1894 by the manufacturer of the Jewett Table Kettle, "to show the great variety of 'elegant and palatable' beverages which can be made by the use of boiling water." Inevitably, most of the recipes are variations of coffee, cocoa, and tea, but the pamphlet also includes some very odd drinks. For instance, Emergency Punch is made with green tea, brandy, rum, Champagne, and Chartreuse, all mixed together and sweetened with a syrup made from oranges, lemons, sugar, water, cloves, and mace. Boiling water is then added "as desired." But this beverage is an emergency in itself! Recommended for those not feeling well (after the crisis or otherwise), Toast Water is made from stale white bread that has been toasted, steeped in boiling water, and strained. The resulting liquid is served with sugar and cream.

An antidote to Toast Water is this Vienna Coffee, with added ice cream. In 1894, ice cream was still a luxury, but in the spirit of Vienna, it surely should be part of this wonderful coffee, hot or cold.

FOR EACH SERVING	3 tablespoons whipped cream
¾ cup chilled coffee	cinnamon
1 scoop vanilla ice cream	

1. Pour chilled coffee into a glass; add ice cream, top with whipped cream, and add a dusting of cinnamon. Serve immediately.

Note: For hot Vienna Coffee, pour hot coffee into a cup or mug; add ice cream, whipped cream, and cinnamon.

One serving

Adapted from "Five O'Clock Tea"
The John C. Jewett Manufacturing Company, 1894

Cranberry Sherbert

Marshwort was once another name for cranberry. Can you imagine eating turkey with marshwort sauce? It is a shame to limit marshworts — or cranberries — to Thanksgiving and Christmas. They can do so much more than accompany a turkey or decorate a tree. Even though they are not available in stores all year, they are easy to freeze. Just take the package out of your grocery bag and put it in the freezer. That's all. Frozen cranberries keep for months, and their sauce is as good in May as it is in November. Fresh or frozen, there are dozens of other lovely things that can be done with cranberries, one of which is cranberry sherbet.

4 cups cranberries
2½ cups cold water plus ½ cup for
 softening the gelatin
2 cups sugar

1 teaspoon unflavored gelatin (⅓ of an
 individual package)
juice of 2 lemons, strained

1. Cook the cranberries and 2½ cups of water in a large saucepan until the berries stop popping, about 10 minutes. Strain, pushing hard with the back of a spoon against the solids in the strainer. Pour the juice back into the saucepan and add the sugar. Cook, stirring, until the sugar is completely dissolved.

2. Sprinkle the gelatin over ½ cup of cold water in a small cup and let sit for 5 minutes, or until the grains are softened and swollen. Add to the hot cranberry juice and stir until completely dissolved. Add the lemon juice.

3. Pour into a freezing pan (a bowl, mold, or pan) and place in the freezer for at least 2 to 3 hours, stirring with a fork or whisk every half hour or so to prevent crystals from forming.

8 servings

Adapted from "Fascinating Cranberries"
Eatmor Cranberries, American Cranberry Exchange,
undated

The HOUSEWIFE'S ALMANAC

A BOOK FOR HOMEMAKERS

★

$\mathcal{F}$ine flavor in fruits is what "good breeding" is in people. One is just as much a matter of careful cultivation as the other. Both are developed only under the most favorable environment.

"Tempting Davis Recipes"
Davis Baking Powder, 1925

$\mathcal{F}ruit\ Desserts$

Apple Custard

*A*pple Custard is not to be confused with custard apple. The latter is a tropical fruit that can be eaten with a spoon and is supposed to taste like custard. Apple Custard tastes exactly like custard because it *is* custard, poured over gently cooked apples and their juice. You can further the gilding process if you like by topping all, according to the pamphlet, with a meringue. I opt for the relative simplicity of cooked sugared apples and custard. It has a very nurturing taste. This is comfort food, pure and not-so-simple.

6 apples (Granny Smith or Golden Delicious)
1 cup sugar plus an additional ¼ cup
1 cup cold water
juice of 1 lemon (about 4 tablespoons)
2 cups milk

1 teaspoon cornstarch
3 egg yolks or 2 whole eggs
pinch of salt
1 teaspoon pure vanilla extract

1. Peel, core, and quarter the apples. Place in a saucepan and add 1 cup of the sugar, water, and lemon juice. Cook, covered, over low heat until the apples are tender but still hold their shape, about 15 minutes. Using a slotted spoon, remove the apple pieces and place them in the bottom of a serving dish.

2. Continue cooking the juice left in the saucepan, over medium-high heat, until it is thick and syrupy, about 15 minutes. Pour over the apples.

3. Mix 1 teaspoon of the milk with the cornstarch to form a thick paste. Heat the remaining milk in a saucepan to the scalding point, when small bubbles form around the edges of the pan. In the meantime, beat the eggs, the remaining $\frac{1}{4}$ cup sugar, and the salt with a whisk until blended. Slowly add the hot milk to the egg mixture, and return to the saucepan. Stir in the cornstarch. Cook over low heat, stirring constantly with a wooden spoon, until the mixture thickens. (175 degrees on a candy thermometer; without a candy thermometer, when steam begins to rise from the pan remove the spoon and run your fingertip down the back of its bowl. If your finger leaves a clear path, the custard is done. What's important is to work quickly, so the eggs don't scramble.) Remove from the heat, cool slightly, and add the vanilla. Pour the cooled custard over the apples. Refrigerate until ready to serve.

6 servings

Adapted from "Davis Cook Book"
Davis Baking Powder, undated, c. 1905

Brown Betty

Brown betties, fools, buckles, grunts, slumps, cobble . . . What strange names some fruit desserts have! What are they? A cobbler is a biscuit-type batter spread over fruit and baked. Slumps are similar, but made with a looser batter — you could say it slumps on the plate. Grunts are another variation, in which the dough steams on the top of the fruit, like a dumpling in a stew — some say it makes grunting sounds as it simmers. Buckles are made with cake batter on the bottom of the pan and fruit on top; while they bake, some of the batter buckles and bubbles up. Fools are not a bit foolish, but they *are* simple: just whipped cream swirled into sweetened and puréed fruit. Brown betties are fruit, usually apples, layered with buttered bread crumbs and baked. I don't know who Betty was, but she was one smart cook.

5 slices firm white bread (like Pepperidge Farm or Arnold)

4 tablespoons unsalted butter plus butter for the baking dish

6 apples

1 teaspoon lemon juice

³/₄ cup sugar

½ teaspoon cinnamon

½ teaspoon nutmeg, freshly grated if possible

1. Preheat the oven to 325 degrees. Butter an 8-inch square baking dish.
2. Blend the bread and butter in a food processor to make buttered bread crumbs. If you don't have a processor, melt the butter in a frying pan and stir in the finely crumbled bread. Place a layer of the crumbs in the baking dish.
3. Peel, core, and quarter the apples, and slice each quarter into quarters. Sprinkle the apples with the lemon juice, and mix to coat. In a separate bowl, combine the sugar, cinnamon, and nutmeg. Place a layer of apples over the bread crumbs and sprinkle with some of the sugar mixture. Add another layer of crumbs, and continue to make alternating layers of apples, sugar, and crumbs, ending with bread crumbs.
4. Bake for 45 minutes, or until the top is browned and the apples are soft. Serve with whipped cream or vanilla ice cream.

6 servings

Adapted from "Good Things to Eat"
Fleischmann Company, 1912

Baked Bananas

We take bananas for granted. Everybody knows what to do with them; you just peel and eat. Once, they were exotic treats, and we had to learn what to do with them. The pamphlet this recipe comes from has a drawing of the ripening stages of bananas. "Yellow ripe bananas," it says, "can be readily digested by any healthy person." And bananas were so luxurious then that all the recipes were created by the former chef to King Albert of Belgium.

IMPORTANT

In preparing bananas for cooking they should always be peeled before using and all coarse threads removed.

"From the Tropics to Your Table"
Fruit Dispatch Company, 1926

We also take bananas for granted by limiting their potential in the kitchen. We eat them raw and we make banana cream pie and banana bread. And then we stop. But there are a zillion things to do with bananas. (Banana Marmalade! Meat Loaf with Bananas! says the King's chef.) Baked Bananas are just the beginning, but they're a fine way to start.

1 tablespoon unsalted butter	6 teaspoons brown sugar
6 bananas	6 tablespoons water

1. Preheat the oven to 350 degrees. Use about a teaspoon of the butter to grease an 8-inch square baking dish.
2. Peel the bananas and slice them in half, lengthwise. Place them in the baking dish. Sprinkle with the sugar and pour the water around them. Dot with the remaining butter.
3. Bake until the bananas are translucent and the sauce is syrupy. Serve with cream, whipped cream, or vanilla ice cream.

Note: Try using orange or apple juice, white wine, or rum instead of water.

6 servings

Adapted from "From the Tropics to Your Table"
Fruit Dispatch Company, 1926

Milton Berle's Peach Cobbler

*I*n 1945, when the "The Cook Book of the Stars" was published, Milton Berle was the side-splitting star of Eversharp's glittering radio show, 'Let Yourself Go!' Before that, he was a vaudeville star, and after that, a television star — everybody's much loved Uncle Miltie, a three-media favorite. If it's hard to think of him cooking up a storm, just imagine a little frilly apron, a semi-circle edged in ruffles, tied around his waist, over his suit jacket. This unusual Peach Cobbler was his contribution to the "Cook Book of the Stars."

2 tablespoons unsalted butter, plus butter for the baking dish
2 15-ounce cans peaches, canned in juice
1 teaspoon cinnamon
½ teaspoon nutmeg
1 8-ounce box corn muffin mix

2 tablespoons sugar
6 tablespoons water
FOR THE SAUCE:
1 cup of juice reserved from the peaches
1 tablespoon cornstarch
1 teaspoon unsalted butter

1. Preheat the oven to 350 degrees. Butter an 8-inch square baking dish.
2. Drain the peaches, reserving the juice. Mix the peaches with the cinnamon and nutmeg and place in the baking dish.
3. Combine the muffin mix with the sugar; cut in the butter, using two knives, a pastry blender, or a food processor. Add the water and stir. The batter will be very thick.
4. Spoon the batter over the peaches, spreading it as evenly as possible — it doesn't have to reach the sides. Bake for 20 minutes, or until the top is well browned.
5. Mix 1 tablespoon of the reserved peach juice with the cornstarch to form a smooth paste. Heat the remaining juice in a saucepan over medium heat, and when it's hot, gradually whisk in the cornstarch mixture. Stir until the sauce thickens. Remove from the heat and stir in the butter.
6. Serve the sauce hot with the warm cobbler. If you want to add a dollop of whipped cream or a scoop of vanilla ice cream, who would stop you?

6 servings

Adapted from "The Cook Book of the Stars"
WFBL, 1945

Roast Peaches

We have grown used to roasted vegetables, with their marvelous colors and deeply intense flavors. But we don't often roast fruits, which is a shame, because the same thing happens to roasted fruits as to vegetables. Flavor intensifies. Roast peaches (or nectarines, pears, or plums) are an excellent example of the process.

unsalted butter for the baking dish
peaches
FOR EACH PEACH:
½ teaspoon white or brown sugar

¼ teaspoon unsalted butter
lemon juice
nutmeg, freshly grated if possible
water or juice (see note)

1. Preheat the oven to 350 degrees. Butter a baking dish large enough to hold the number of peaches you are using.
2. Peel the peaches by dipping them into boiling water for 10 seconds; remove them, and immediately plunge them into very cold water. The skins should slip off easily. Halve the peaches and remove the pits.
3. Place the peaches, pitted side up, in the baking dish. Fill each cavity with a mixture of the sugar, butter, a few drops of lemon juice, and a sprinkle of nutmeg. Add water or juice to the baking dish to a depth of about ½ inch.
4. Bake for 30 to 45 minutes, until the peaches are lightly browned. Serve hot with plain or whipped cream, or vanilla ice cream.

Note: Use apple, peach, or pear juice, or any other juice (or wine) you prefer.

Adapted from "Kerr Home Canning Book"
Kerr Glass Mfg. Corp., 1943

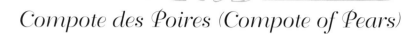

Compote des Poires (Compote of Pears)

A compote is a dessert of fruit gently cooked in a sugar syrup and flavored with cinnamon or vanilla. We don't often get excited about compotes, perhaps because we tend to think of them as a winter dessert, a make-do of dried fruit cooked in syrup, a wintry reminder of summer's bounty. But compotes made with fresh fruit are simple to prepare, elegant to behold, and refreshing to eat — worth getting excited about. There are good reasons why compotes are classic French desserts. This compote is made with pears, but similar steps could be used for peaches, plums, nectarines, berries — almost any fruit, and it would still be called a compote or simply poached fruit. And it would still be lovely

6 pears
cold water
freshly squeezed lemon
  juice
2 cups sugar
1 stick cinnamon

DELECTABLE FRUIT COMPOTE

1. Peel the pears, leaving them whole but keeping their stems attached. As you peel each pear, drop it into a bowl of cold water mixed with a few drops of lemon juice.

2. Combine the sugar and 1 cup fresh, cold water in a large saucepan and bring to a boil. Lower the heat and simmer for 8 minutes. Add the cinnamon stick. Drain the pears and add them to the hot syrup. Cover and cook gently for 15 to 20 minutes, until the pears are tender but not mushy. Remove them from the syrup and place them, with their stems upright, in a large bowl.

3. Continue to cook the poaching liquid until it thickens and becomes syrupy. Cool slightly, and then pour over the pears. Serve at room temperature or chilled.

6 servings

Adapted from "Around the World Cook Book"
Kalamazoo Stove and Furnace Company, 1951

Pear Trifle

A trifle is an inconsequential thing, something that doesn't matter very much. But when it's a dessert, a trifle is much greater than the sum of its small parts: cake, custard, fruit, jam, and sherry, all slathered with whipped cream and carefully layered in a big glass bowl. A 1755 recipe includes biscuits, ratafias, macaroons, sack, and custard, all covered with syllabub. It's described as "fit to go to the King's table." This is a simple, more democratic trifle, and while it may be a tiny bit — just a trifle — unorthodox, it is still, in its way, elaborate. No sensible king would pass it up.

2 cups milk

3 egg yolks or 2 whole eggs

¼ cup sugar

pinch of salt

1 teaspoon pure vanilla extract

12 slices pound cake (fresh or frozen)

6 pears, peeled, cored, halved, and lightly poached, or canned in their own juice

1 cup heavy cream, whipped

optional garnish: unsalted shelled pistachio nuts or candied fruit

1. Make a custard sauce by heating the milk in a medium-sized saucepan to the scalding point, when small bubbles form around the edge of the pan. Meanwhile, in a separate bowl, whisk the eggs, sugar, and salt together until thoroughly blended. Gradually pour the hot milk into the egg mixture, whisking constantly. Then pour the mixture back into the saucepan. Cook over low heat, stirring constantly with a wooden spoon, until the mixture thickens. (175 degrees on a candy thermometer; without a candy thermometer, when steam begins to rise from the pan remove the spoon and run your fingertip down the back of its bowl. If your finger leaves a clear path, the custard is done. What's important is to work quickly, so the eggs don't scramble.) Immediately remove from the heat and allow to cool. Stir in the vanilla.

2. Place the slices of pound cake on a serving plate, and top each slice with a pear half. (Cut a thin slice off the rounded side of the pear halves so they'll stay flat.) Pour the custard sauce over the pears and cake. Decorate with the whipped cream, and, if you like, scatter the nuts or fruits (or both!) on top.

6 to 12 servings

Adapted from "The Del Monte Fruit Book"
California Packing Corporation, 1926

Shortcakes, Strawberry and Otherwise

Strawberry shortcake is as American as apple pie, even though both apple pie and shortcake were originally English. No matter. Shortcake is now an American classic. It frequently gets confused with short*bread*, which is a buttery cookie, and with just plain cake. Shortcake is short — not in height, silly, but in crispness — because it's made with butter (or lard or vegetable shortening, depending on your heritage). In fact, a shortcake is a biscuit, sweetened because it's being used as a dessert. It is delicious, delightful, and delovely made with strawberries, but it's just as good and more surprising made with sliced peaches, pitted cherries, blueberries, raspberries, sliced plums, nectarines . . . Happy thoughts, all.

I feel sure no one would ever serve a makeshift shortcake with sponge cake if they knew how easy it is to make the real thing with perfect biscuits.

"Be an Artist at the Gas Range" The Mystery Chef and Your Gas Company, 1935

5 tablespoons unsalted butter, plus butter
   for the baking pan
2 cups flour
4 teaspoons baking powder
½ teaspoon salt
2 tablespoons sugar

¾ to 1 cup milk
fruit and sugar (1 quart strawberries,
   for example, and ½ cup brown
   or white sugar)
1 cup heavy cream, whipped

1. Preheat the oven to 400 degrees. Butter an 8-inch cake pan or a cookie sheet.

2. Combine the flour, baking powder, salt, and sugar in a food processor or mixing bowl. Either cut in the butter, using a pastry blender, two knives, or your fingers, or pulse briefly to combine. Add the milk, as much as needed (usually, depending on the humidity, among other things, just under a cup) to make a dough that barely holds together. Either turn into the cake pan and pat into

shape, or roll out on a lightly floured board and use a biscuit cutter or the floured rim of a glass to make 2-inch biscuits. (Try to work quickly with the dough and to use a minimum of flour while rolling it out, to keep the biscuits tender.) Place the biscuits on the cookie sheet.

3. Bake for 15 to 20 minutes, until golden brown.

4. Remove from the oven, and split in half horizontally. (Some people like to butter their shortcakes. This is entirely up to you.)

5. While the shortcakes are baking, prepare the fruit. Slice a quart of strawberries, leaving 12 whole. Add the sugar (tasting to see if more is needed) to the berries and let stand until juice forms. At serving time (the shortcakes should be warm — reheat in the oven briefly if you have to), spoon dollops of strawberries and juice on the bottom layers of the short-cakes, cover with the tops, and add more strawberries over all. Top with whipped cream, and, for each serving, 2 whole strawberries.

Note: Prepare other fruits in the same way. Peel and pit peaches, nectarines, or plums, slice thinly, mix with sugar, and let stand to make juice. Raspberries can be mixed with sugar just as the strawberries are, but without slicing. Blueberries are wonderful if some of them are stewed briefly with a bit of sugar (add a little cinnamon or freshly grated nutmeg if you like); then combine the cooked and cooled blueberries with fresh whole berries to serve. Another way of serving shortcake is to present the parts — biscuits, fruit, and whipped cream — in separate bowls and let your guests help themselves.

6 servings

Adapted from "Be an Artist at the Gas Range"
The Mystery Chef and Your Gas Company, 1935

*I*f you were to ask me how to give a "professional touch" to your every-day desserts, I should tell you not to bother preparing *elaborate dishes* at all, but to go straight along with your gelatines and tapiocas,

fruits, berries, puddings and pastries; *looking to your sauces!* Chances are, your desserts, excellent in themselves, are eloquently

Frostings and Sauces

incomplete for want of an appropriate sauce to "dress them up!"

And there is the whole secret of the *fine art* of dessert making!

"Hip-O-Lite Recipes"
Marshmallow Cream, undated

Cream Cheese Date-Nut Frosting

*I*n the 1960s, cream cheese frosting became wildly popular on carrot cake, almost a dessert emblem of the flower children's generation. They have long since grown up, but cream cheese frosting is as fresh and good as ever. Here, the cream cheese is mixed with dates and nuts to make a sort of creamy variation of old-fashioned date-nut bread. The frosting is still lovely on carrot cake, or gingerbread, or pound cake, or any number of cakes. It's even good on toast.

8 ounces cream cheese at room temperature	1½ teaspoons pure vanilla extract
½ cup unsalted butter at room temperature	4 tablespoons chopped dates
4 cups confectioners' sugar	4 tablespoons chopped pecans, walnuts
	optional: raisins or crystallized ginger
	small pinch of salt

1. Cream the cheese and butter together until the mixture is smooth. Gradually add the sugar. Add the vanilla, continuing to beat. Finally, add the dates, nuts (and raisins or ginger, if using) and salt. If the frosting is too thick, add a bit of milk or cream, a teaspoon at a time. If it's too thin, add more sugar very gradually. After frosting the cake, refrigerate until serving, especially in warm weather.

Yield: frosting
to cover an
8-inch cake

Adapted from "Be
an Artist at the
Gas Range"

The Mystery Chef
and Your Gas
Company, 1935

Sour Cream Frosting

I had a friend who thought there were very few things in this world that would not be improved by a tablespoon of sour cream. I agree. Sour cream is not too far away from French crème fraîche. A quick approximation can be made by mixing sour and sweet cream. The classic recipe for making crème fraîche (when you are not in France and can't get the real thing) calls for adding a bit of buttermilk to sweet cream and letting it stand. This works, but it's very slow, while mixing sweet and sour cream is instant. Crème fraîche, like sour cream, is one of many bacterial gifts to the world, offsetting the bacterial curses as good fairies counter the bad. The tang of sour cream in frosting is a nice balance to the deep sweetness of confectioners' sugar.

4 tablespoons unsalted butter

2 cups confectioners' sugar

4 tablespoons sour cream

½ teaspoon pure vanilla extract

small pinch of salt

1. Cream the butter until it's light. Gradually add the sugar. When the mixture is smooth, add the sour cream, vanilla, and salt, and beat well.

Note: The frosting can be decorated with grated orange or lime zest scattered over the top, both as decoration and as flavoring.

Variation: You can easily make coconut frosting by adding shredded coconut to this recipe, and patting more coconut onto the sides of the frosted cake.

Yield: frosting to cover an 8-inch cake

Adapted from "Almanac and Cook Book"
Rumford Chemical Works, 1884

Chocolate Buttercream Frosting

*T*he story of Hershey's chocolate is a saga of hard work and determination. The story of Baker Chocolate is a love story, an especially sweet chocolate tale. According to this Baker pamphlet, there was Prince Ditrichstein, a "brilliant young Austrian nobleman," and there was a waitress in a Viennese chocolate shop, Babette Baldauf, "daughter of an impoverished knight." One frosty afternoon in 1760, the Prince ventured into the shop to try the new drink from Central America that everyone was talking about: hot chocolate. What he found was the prettiest girl in all Vienna. Every day, he came back to drink hot chocolate and enjoy Babette's demure glances. "He completely forgets that a Prince may not look at a waitress . . . ." As a wedding gift, he commissioned a painting of his beloved in her waitressing dress. I don't know whether they lived happily ever after, but the portrait was displayed for many years in the Dresden Museum, and its replica, "La Belle Chocolatierre," became the Baker Chocolate logo. It can still be seen on cans of Walter Baker's Breakfast Cocoa.

1½ squares (1½ ounces) unsweetened chocolate

4 tablespoons unsalted butter

2 cups confectioners' sugar

¾ teaspoon pure vanilla extract

4 teaspoons milk or cream, or as needed

1. In a small saucepan over very low heat, melt the chocolate. Cool slightly.
2. Cream the butter until it's smooth and light; gradually add one cup of the sugar, continuing to beat. Add the vanilla and the melted chocolate. Beat well. Add the remaining sugar, beating well. Add the milk gradually, adding more if needed to reach the consistency for spreading.

Variations: Orange Butter Frosting: Omit the chocolate, vanilla, and milk. Instead, add the grated zest of one orange, ½ teaspoon orange extract, and 3 tablespoons orange juice. *Coffee Butter Frosting:* Omit the chocolate and milk. Instead, add ½ teaspoon cocoa and 3 to 4 tablespoons strong coffee. *Mocha Butter Frosting:* Omit the milk and instead add the same quantity of strong coffee.

Yield: frosting to cover an 8-inch cake

Adapted from "Best Chocolate Recipes"
Walter Baker & Company, Inc., 1932

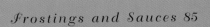

Chocolate Sauce

I love vanilla ice cream, and I don't often see any point in covering it with anything. Why lose the pure, clean, cold, sweet dairy taste of vanilla and cream? But chocolate sauce over vanilla ice cream is an entirely different proposition. When the chocolate sauce is hot and the ice cream begins to melt under it, they merge into a luscious chocolatey cream. When the chocolate sauce is cold, the pleasures are separate. Together, the combination is reminiscent of such a simple joy as chocolate milk, all grown up now and turned into frozen cream. What bliss it all is, to have such choices!

3 squares (3 ounces) unsweetened chocolate
½ cup milk
¾ cup sugar

1 tablespoon unsalted butter
pinch of salt
¾ teaspoon pure vanilla extract

1. Melt the chocolate with the milk in a small saucepan over very low heat, stirring occasionally, until the chocolate is completely melted and the mixture is very smooth. Add the sugar and continue to cook until it's dissolved; add the butter and salt and cook for 3 to 5 minutes longer, until slightly thickened.

2. Remove from the heat. Let cool slightly and stir in the vanilla. Serve hot or cold.

Note: The sauce thickens as it stands, and becomes almost solid when it's refrigerated. It can be thinned with milk or cream. If you need to reheat it, either use a double boiler or heat it gently over low heat. In addition to ice cream, chocolate sauce can adorn a variety of desserts: cakes and some fruits and berries. Try it with strawberries, for instance — they're especially good with chocolate sauce.

Yield: 1½ cups

Adapted from "New Ways with Ice Cream"
Sealtest, Inc., 1949

Strawberry Sauce

"**D**oubtless God could have made a better berry," William Butler wrote, "but doubtless God never did." This is the famous quote about strawberries, and it's not far off the mark, depending on your taste for raspberries and blueberries. Once, we had to wait until spring to eat strawberries. They were all the more precious because they were seasonal. Now, they're available year-round in stores, frozen or shipped fresh from other regions. Strawberry sauce stretches their goodness, and makes a variety of other things happy, from ice cream to cheesecake to other berries.

1 quart strawberries, hulled and rinsed (see note)
1 cup sugar
optional: lemon juice (see note)

1. Place the strawberries in a bowl, pour the sugar over them, mix very gently and let stand for 1 hour.
2. Mash the strawberries lightly.
3. Put the berries into a saucepan over low heat, and cook gently just until they reach the boiling point. Remove from the heat. Serve hot or cold.

Note: The original recipe indicates that blackberry, raspberry, or peach sauce may be prepared using the same method. With any of these fruits, including strawberries, a few drops of lemon juice before or after cooking helps to accent the flavor. Note too that there isn't anybody who could tell you that these strawberries aren't perfectly delicious *without* being cooked, especially with a little cream or yogurt or sour cream.

Yield: about 4 cups

Adapted from "Davis Cook Book"
Davis Baking Powder, c. 1905

Whipped Cream Sauces

*I*s it possible to grow tired of whipped cream? No. But, just for a change, on a quiet day, there are other things that can be done with a cup of heavy cream. It depends on your mood, the state of your pantry, and what will be going under the cream. But whatever you do with it, whipped cream is always there for you.

Chocolate Whipped Cream

Whip 1 cup heavy cream until soft peaks form. Add 2 tablespoons chocolate syrup and whip until stiff.

Adapted from "Fifty-five Recipes"
Hershey Chocolate Corporation, undated

Cinnamon Whipped Cream

Lovely with baked apples.
Whip ¾ cup heavy cream until soft peaks form. Add 1½ tablespoons powdered sugar and ¾ teaspoon cinnamon. Whip until stiff.

Adapted from "The Sealtest Food Adviser"
Sealtest, Inc., 1939

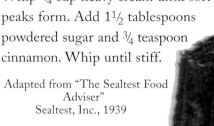

Chocolate Walnut Cream

Good with cake.

Heat 1 square (1 ounce) unsweetened chocolate and ¾ cup milk in the top of a double boiler and beat until thoroughly combined. In a separate bowl, combine 6 tablespoons sugar, 2 tablespoons cake flour, and a pinch of salt, and gradually add this mixture to the chocolate. Cook until thickened, stirring constantly. Cook 5 minutes longer, stirring occasionally. Add 1 tablespoon butter, cool slightly, and add 1 teaspoon vanilla. Chill. Whip 1 cup heavy cream. Fold the whipped cream and ½ cup chopped walnuts into the chocolate sauce.

Adapted from "Cake Secrets"
Swans Down Cake Flour, 1941

Coffee Whipped Cream

This is as good as the coffee you make it with, and at its best, it is absolutely delicious. Using gelatin results in whipped cream that will hold its shape, even in warm weather. Excellent with chocolate ice cream or cake.

Sprinkle ½ teaspoon gelatin over 2 tablespoons strong coffee in a cup. Let stand 5 minutes. Place the cup in a pan of very hot water and stir the gelatin until it dissolves. Whip 1 cup heavy cream with 2 tablespoons sugar and ¼ teaspoon pure vanilla extract until soft peaks form. Add the gelatin mixture and 2 additional tablespoons coffee and whip until stiff.

Adapted from "Coffee or Tea?"
Maxwell House, undated, c. 1920

Art Credits

"Bananas in the Modern Manner," Banana Growers Association, New York, NY. 1930. 14, 15.

"Bananas Take a Bow," Meloripe Fruit Company, Boston, MA. Undated. 8.

"Birds Eye Cook Book," Frosted Foods Sales Corp. 1941. 10.

"Borden's Eagle Brand Book of Recipes," The Borden Company, NY. Undated.Title, 49, 78, 88.

"Borden's Evaporated Milk Book of Recipes," The Borden Company, NY. Undated. Cover, 9, 56.

"Cake Secrets," Igleheart Bros. 1919. Cover (three), 13.

"Cake Secrets," Igleheart Brothers, Inc., Evansville, IN. 1928. 22, 25.

"The Calumet Baking Book," Calumet Baking Powder Co. 1931. Jacket, Cover, 13, 81 (three).

"Calumet Cook Book," Calumet Baking Powder Co., Chicago, IL. Undated. Cover.

"Ceresota Cook Book," The Northwestern Consolidated Milling Co., Minneapolis, MN. Undated. Cover (two).

"Cheese and Ways to Serve It," Kraft-Phenix Cheese Corporation, Chicago, Il. 1931. 20.

"Choice Recipes " Walter Baker & Co., Ltd. Dorchester, MA. 1901. Title page.

"Choice Recipes," Walter Baker & Co., Ltd., Dorchester, MA. 1916. 84.

"Cocoa and Chocolate," Walter Baker & Co., Ltd., Dorchester, MA. 1917. 39.

"Condensed Milk," NY Condensed Milk, New York, NY. 1887. 86.

"A Cookery Expert's New Recipes," Hershey Chocolate Company, Hershey, PA. Undated. 36.

"The Cream Top Book of Tested Recipes," Cream Top Bottle Corporation, Albany, NY. Undated. 55.

"Dainty Desserts for Dainty People," Charles B. Knox, Johnstown, NY. 1901. 3 (two), 44.

"Decorate Your Own Cakes," Woman's Home Companion, 1926. 83.

"Delightful Cooking," Corn Products Refining Co., New York, NY. Undated. 44.

"Del Monte Fruit Book," California Packing Corporation, San Francisco, CA. 1926. 8.

"Discovered," The Club Aluminum Company, Chicago, IL. Undated. 64.

"Douglas Oil for Best Salads and Better Cooking," Douglas Company, Cedar Rapids, IA. 1918. 53.

"Downright Delicious," Sun-Maid Raisin Growers, Fresno, CA. Undated. Cover, 24.

"Electric Cookery by Hotpoint," Edison General Electric Appliance Co., Inc., Chicago, IL. Undated. 48, 60.

"Favorite Recipes of the Movie Stars," Tower Books, New York, NY. 1931. 54.

"Frigidaire Recipes," Frigidaire Corporation, Dayton, OH. 1929. 6, 63.

"Food Surprises," The Mirro Test Kitchen. Undated. Jacket, 47 (two), 72.

"Getting the Most out of Foods," Corning Glass Works, Corning, NY. Undated. 30.

"Gold Medal Flour Cook Book," Washburn-Crosby Co., Minneapolis, MN. 1910. 43.

"Good Pies," Merrell-Soule Company, Syracuse, NY. Undated. 40, 42.

"Healthful Living," Battle Creek Food Company, Battle Creek, MI. Undated. 10.

"Henry's Cook Book and Household Companion," John E. Henry & Co., New York, NY. Jacket.

"Hershey's Recipes" Hershey Chocolate Corporation, Hershey, PA. Cover, Borders, 12, 38.

"Home Baked Delicacies, Igleheart Brothers, Evansville, IN. 1929. 85.

"Hotpoint Electric Cooking and Home Canning Book," Edison General Electric Appliance Company, Inc., Chicago, IL. Undated. Jacket (spine), 16, 46, 76.

"The Housewive's Almanac," Kellogg Company, Battle Creek, MI. 1938. 68.

"How to Make Tempting Nutritious Desserts," Hansen's Laboratory, Inc., Little Falls, NY. 1941. 4.

"Jell-O, America's Most Famous Dessert," The Genesee Pure Food Co., Le Roy, NY. Undated. 62

"The Jell-O Girl Entertains," The Jell-O Company, Inc., Le Roy, NY. Undated. Cover (two).

"Jell-O, Quick Easy Wonder Dishes," The Jell-O Company, Inc., Le Roy, NY. Undated. 5, 57.

"The Latest Cake Secrets," General Foods Corporation, New York, NY. 1934. 21, 75, 80.

"Lilly of the Valley," Winters & Prophet Canning Co., Rochester, NY.1925. 69.

"Maxwell House: Coffee or Tea?" Cheek-Neal Coffee Co. Undated. 31.

"Menu Magic in a Nutshell," California Walnut Growers Association, Los Angeles, CA. Cover.

"Monarch Cook Book," Malleable Iron Range Co., Beaver Damn, WI. 6.

"Nabisco," National Biscuit Company. Undated. 2.

"New Magic in the Kitchen," The Borden Company, New York, NY. Undated. 70.

"New Party Cakes," General Mills, Inc., Minneapolis, MN. 1931. 19.

"New Perfection Cook Book," The Cleveland Foundry Co. 1912. 5.

"Original Menus," Curtice Brothers Co., Rochester, NY. 1908. Title, Contents, 7.

"Proven Recipes," Corn Products Refining Co., New York, NY. 17.

"Pyrex Experts Book on Better Cooking," Corning Glass Works, Corning, NY. 1924. Cover.

"Recipe and Instruction Book," Hamilton Beach Mixette, Racine,WI. Cover, 33.

"Reliable Recipes and Helpful Hints," Calumet Baking Powder, Chicago, IL. Undated. 28.

"Royal Baker and Pastry Cook," Royal Baking Powder Co., New York, NY. Undated. 45, 52.

"Royal Desserts Recipes," Standard Brands Incorporated, 1940. 11.

"Rumford Fruit Cook Book," Rumford Company, Providence, RI, 1927. Cover (two), 29, 58, 71.

"The School Lunch," Postum Co, Inc., New York, NY. 1928. 35.

"Secrets of Coffee Flavor," Cheek-Neal Coffee Company, 1927. 65.

"The Silent Servant," B.T.H. Electric Refrigerator, Undated. 59, 67.

"Sunkist Orange Recipes," California Fruit Growers Exchange, Los Angeles, CA, 1940. Cover, 34.

"Super Chief Cook Book," Santa Fe Lines, Undated. 23.

"Unusual Recipes," Borden's Condensed Milk Company, New York, NY, 1911. 66.

"Washington Flour," Wilkins-Rogers Milling Co., Washington D.C., Undated. 26.

"WFBL Cook Book of the Stars," Onondaga Radio Broadcasting Corp., Syracuse, NY, 1945. 74.

"What Shall I Cook Today?," Lever Brothers Company, Cambridge, MA, Undated. 79.

"A Year of Recipes," Abbott Dairies, Inc. 1933. 61.

"Your Share," General Mills, 1943. 77.

Bibliography

Ayto, John, *The Diner's Dictionary; Food and Drink from A to Z.* Oxford University Press, 1993.

Bloom , Carole, *The International Dictionary of Desserts, Pastries, and Confections.* Hearst Books, 1995.

Claiborne, Craig, *The New York Times Food Encyclopedia.* Times Books, 1985.

Cowan, Ruth Schwartz, *More Work for Mother: The Ironies of Household Technology from the Open Hearth to the Microwave.* Basic Books, Inc., 1983.

Jones, Evan, *American Food: The Gastronomic Story.* E. P. Dutton, 1975.

Levenstein, Harvey, *Revolution at the Table.* Oxford University Press, 1988.

Mariani, John F., *The Dictionary of American Food.* Hearst Books, 1994.

Plante, Ellen M., *The American Kitchen 1700 to the Present: From Hearth to Highrise.* Facts on File, 1995.

Shapiro, Laura, *Perfection Salad: Women and Cooking at the Turn of the Century.* Farrar, Straus and Giroux, 1986

Trager, James, *The Enriched Fortified Concentrated Country-Fresh Lip-Smacking Finger-Licking International Unexpurgated Foodbook.* Grossman Publishers, 1970.

Trager, James, *The Food Chronology.* Henry Holt, 1995.

Index